THE FERRARI

Library of Congress Cataloging in Publication Data

Rogliatti, Gianni.
   The Ferrari.

   1. Ferrari automobile.   I. Title.
TL215.F47R6313   629.22′8   73–1018
ISBN 0–690–29603–7

THE FERRARI

by Gianni Rogliatti

Thomas Y. Crowell Company

New York • Established 1834

This is the
first time that
the fruit of twenty-five years
of my work
has been described
faithfully and substantially.

ENZO FERRARI

PART ONE

History of the Firm

Enzo Ferrari and His Team	11
Maranello	17
A Quarter of a Century of Improvements	25
. . . and Then Came Fiat	35

PART TWO

Production

Model 125 S	40
Model 166 S	46
Model 125 F1	53
Model 212 Export	60
Model 375 F1	65
Model 500 F2	72
Model 340 S	80
Model 342 America	85
Model 250 Europa	88
Model 375 MM	92
Model 625 F1	101
Model 750 Monza	109
Model 410 Superamerica	116
Model 290 MM	120
Model 246 F1	124
Model 250 TRS	132
Model 250 GT	136
Model 400 Superamerica	140
Model 156 F1	144
Model 246 P	153
Model 250 GTO	160
Model 250 LM	164
Model 330 GT 2 + 2	168
Model 158 F1	173
Model 500 Superfast	180
Model 275 GTS — GTB	184
Model 330 P2 — P3 — P4	189
Model 206 Dino	196
Model 312 B	205
Model 312 P	216
Model 512 S	220
Model 365 GTC 4	231
Summary of Ferrari Production	241

PART ONE

HISTORY OF THE FIRM

Acerbo Cup, 1936: Nuvolari refreshes himself after the victory. Enzo Ferrari is at the left.

ENZO FERRARI AND HIS TEAM

In the hectic seventies, when nearly everything seems to become obsolete overnight, it is almost impossible to imagine one man being a fixture in the automobile world for more than fifty years. That is why Enzo Ferrari has become a legend in his own time. The history of Italian sports cars is stamped with his personality and, deservedly, his influence has grown internationally year by year and his name continues to shine ever more brightly, perhaps more than any other automobile great, past or present. Say "Ferrari" and you conjure up something exciting and memorable.

Enzo Ferrari was born in Modena on February 20, 1898. Practically as a child he watched the early development of the automobile and heard about such exploits as Prince Scipione Borghese winning the Peking-Paris endurance run. These adventures were typical of the period but, in themselves, are not enough to explain a career. Evidently Ferrari was born with a special gift for leadership and invention; even today he likes to speak of his ability to fire up other men. In this respect he is an "agitator."

He had a normal upbringing in the provinces and, even before he was old enough to get a license, easily learned to drive the rattletrap cars of the period. He did get a license at eighteen, but World War I was on and he had no occasion to use it. As might be expected he was mobilized into the Alpine or mountain infantry, where he had to care for mules rather than cars and trucks.

His incredible climb to the top began just after the war. In 1919 he hurried to Turin, which was already the mecca of Italian motoring. But post-World War I Turin was far different from today's industrial capital and when Ferrari sought work at the Fiat plant, he was turned down flat. It was a disillusioning experience—a hurt and a slight he never forgave or forgot.

In his book *Le mie gioie terribili* (*My Terrible Joys*) he tells how completely alone he felt, suddenly broke, friendless, and jobless. He was so depressed that he slumped on a bench in Valentino Park, close by the Fiat plant, and wept. It is hard to say whether this Dickensian tableau provoked his determination to become big enough in his own right to shake the power of Fiat, but it is certain that the bench in Valentino Park provided a launching pad for his career. He finally found work in a small local machine shop and stayed there a year before moving on to Alfa Romeo in Milan. Here for twenty years (1920–40) he had every conceivable job: desk clerk, mechanic, test driver, racing driver, sports director, technical and commercial consultant, and creator of the famous Ferrari team, which was the Alfa Romeo racing group and the forerunner of all modern racing teams.

Ferrari first got even with Fiat in 1923 when he managed to talk Vittorio Jano into working for Alfa Romeo. For Fiat, Jano had just finished preparing the 805 racing car, with eight cylinders in line and a compressor. The car was clear proof that he was the most brilliant racing-car designer of the time.

Fiat abandoned competition, and Jano built for Alfa Romeo a revised and improved model of the Fiat 805 —the Alfa P2—which was to head off all rivals for the next ten years. Clearly Ferrari had already begun to fire up his associates. The Ferrari team was officially founded in 1929, and the story back of its insignia is well known by now. The rearing pony on a yellow background was formerly the cockpit emblem of Baracca, an Italian World War I air ace, and was given to Ferrari, who had been one of his admirers, by the flier's parents. The yellow of the background was the official color of Modena.

The Ferrari team reads like the Almanach de Gotha of sports-car racing—Ascari the elder, Campari, Tadini, Arcangeli, Nuvolari, Varzi, Moll, Brivio, Caracciola, Farina. Not that the Alfa Romeos were unbeatable. Even the genius of Jano, and the ingenuity of Ferrari and of the loyal Bazzi, had to give way now and then to powerful German cars by Mercedes and Auto Union. These defeats led to the design of a twin-engine Alfa, but with indifferent results. Still they never lost hope, never stopped trying. For Ferrari nothing could be worse than that park bench in Turin—not the defeats, the failures, the crushing loss of drivers who were close friends as well as colleagues, the carping critics, the bitter personal attacks.

As a driver Ferrari held his own, no more, winning twelve races from 1921 to 1931, but he competed only sporadically because he was too involved in other activities of the firm. Still his limited racing experience provided him with invaluable firsthand knowledge of the racing driver's unpredictable world.

Along with his many other jobs he became a writer and editor, publishing a magazine for clients and friends of the Ferrari team which still appears annually, and writing two autobiographical books.

With the adoption of a new formula limiting cylinder capacity to 1.5 liters (1,500 cubic centimeters = 1,500 cm³; about a quart and a half), another masterpiece emerged in 1937: the famous Alfetta 158, conceived by Ferrari and designed by Gioacchino Colombo, Bazzi, Nasi, and Gilberti with the cooperation, at a later stage, of Massimino. However, the 158 program suddenly changed when, that same year, Alfa Romeo suddenly decided to absorb the Ferrari team, although keeping its creator as director.

This final phase lasted only till 1940, when Ferrari once and for all left the firm he was to call his "mother house" to set up shop on his own. It was at this time that the first *real* Ferrari was born, but the name could not be officially used for five years because of a contract clause with Alfa Romeo.

Whatever caused the rift, it must have been most serious. In his memoirs Ferrari only mentions a disagreement with a nameless Alfa Romeo Spanish technician who wore shoes with unusually thick rubber soles . . .

The first Ferrari was called Auto Avio Costruzioni model 815; its relation to the Alfa Romeo 158 was all too obvious. They had the same specifications; 158 and 815 indicate the same characteristics, 8 cylinders and a

Enzo Ferrari in his racing debut. Above, at the Targa Florio, driving a CMN; below, Ferrari as a member of the Alfa Romeo team (fifth from the right). On the next page, above, Enzo Ferrari at the wheel of an Alfa Romeo; below left, Count Carlo Felice Trossi at the wheel of a one-seater Duesenberg bought by the Ferrari team; right, Enzo Ferrari in an Alfa Romeo after joining that team.

capacity of 1,500 cm³. But unlike the Alfetta, which was a one-seater, the 815, built with more modest means, was a sports car. Two 815s took part in the 1940 Mille Miglia, driven by the Marquis Lotario Rangoni and young Alberto Ascari, son of Antonio Ascari. The outbreak of World War II prevented the realization of the new, perfected 815 B model on which Massimino had worked and which had a new engine measuring 63 × 60 mm (at first 60 × 66 mm), and two camshafts high in the block. This car preserved the lightness and maneuverability that were typical of the first model: including fuel and two drivers, it weighed only 875 kilograms (less than a ton).

During the war Ferrari built precision milling machines with hydraulic drive, but his factory in Modena was bombed and he decided to move to Maranello, where he owned some land. Here he pondered the relaunching of his old Ferrari team.

He had been married in 1932 and had a son named Alfredo, or "Dino" for short, after Ferrari's older brother. He had great hopes for his son, never dreaming that fate had decided otherwise. Dino died in 1956, shortly after his twenty-fourth birthday. But his name remained linked to an entire epoch in the recent history of the automobile, and with thousands of cars produced not only by Ferrari but now by Fiat.

As for Ferrari, you could write a book on the man's personality and the anecdotes about his life. The judgments in such a book might clash stridently with those of the reader, depending on whether the author was a fanatic admirer or a diehard detractor. A man of the purest genius or just clever and lucky? A man of the greatest sensitivity or absolutely heartless? Shy or selfish, brave or a coward? All these qualities with their corresponding defects could be ascribed to Ferrari to paint either a positive or a negative picture.

For example, let's look at one of his best-known practices: now, since he no longer directs his team personally, he has stopped going to the tracks to watch the cars compete. You might believe his own explanation: that it is painful for him to see men and machines take terrible risks. Or you might have the impression that he disdains participating personally in the fortunes of the drivers and racing thunderbolts to which he has dedicated his life.

And then there is the Ferrari legend. For more than forty years he has never gone to a movie, never taken a vacation, spending his Sundays and holidays at his Maranello studio behind his drafting board. Since the end of the war he has never gone abroad and only on rare occasions has he slept anywhere but in his own home. He is a nonsmoker and eats and drinks little, but it is not clear whether this is from personal inclination or doctor's orders. He reads a great deal, however, in fact all the newspapers he can lay his hands on, and seems to know everything or almost everything about everybody.

Embarkation of the Ferrari team at Genoa in 1936 for the Vanderbilt Cup competition.

Thus described, Ferrari may appear to be almost inhuman, a sort of robot, but this is an inaccurate portrait. Though the passing years have calmed his fiery temperament and, you might say, have drawn a patina of diplomacy over his impetuous spirit, he has been and remains a fighter and an incurable polemicist. In fact he is so fond of argument that from time to time he says or does things that are without rhyme or reason from a practical point of view. Yet when he mentions those who attack him, no matter how unjustly, he often says he couldn't care less; on the contrary, he prefers it because the more violent their broadsides the more he is amused.

From this standpoint the newsmen who interest him most are not those who sing his praises, but those who run him down and with whom he can have a heated argument. Even when he is not assailed in the press, he manages to find topics which leave him room to inveigh against sports authorities, politicians, and a host of others.

Does this mean he has a persecution complex? Not at all, he knows how to play the game of life far too well. As a result, if one of his trusted employees should quit, perhaps to go to a rival firm, he is the first to point out that he, Ferrari, invented this business of walking off with a plant's best technicians. The innumerable storms that have broken over his head appear to have left no trace; he looks at least ten years younger than he is.

In the light of subsequent events, his masterstroke of diplomacy was his accord with Fiat. Thanks to this agreement he not only guaranteed the continuity of the Ferrari name, since no heirs bear it, but at the same time managed the shift from the deliberate craftsmanship production of yesterday to the industrial production of today.

That last-ditch about-face of his, when the contract with Ford needed only his signature—was that all part of a preestablished plan? We shall never know, even though the Ford officials directly concerned in Ferrari negotiations remain convinced that if Henry Ford II in person had gone to Maranello he would have clinched the agreement with a handshake. In any case the result was a blessing for Ferrari and for Italian industry as a whole, which narrowly escaped losing a vital reservoir and an even richer inheritance of experience and high-level technology.

Model 125 S

Model 166 S

Model 125 F1

Model 212 Export

16

Model 375 F1

Model 500 F2

Model 340 S

Model 342 America

MARANELLO

Maranello is a modest little town with a few factories on the Abetone state highway. It is surrounded by a fertile, carefully farmed countryside, but it never could have aspired to fame had it not been picked by chance as the new location for an enterprise which in 1943, in the middle of the war, could easily have ended as a pile of rubble.

The Ferrari plant lies a short distance outside the residential district. Across from it is the famous Cavallino restaurant (the name comes from the Ferrari insignia of a rearing pony against a yellow background), which serves as a lunchroom for virtually all Ferrari employees, and where the curious tourist can eat next to some of the most famous drivers or technicians in the world of car racing.

The original layout of the plant was triangular, extending over a surface of 100,000 square feet, with a courtyard in the center. This same general layout still exists, but after 1961 a new 70,000-square-foot building was added to house the mass production department. In 1970 this department was enlarged with a new wing of an additional 100,000 square feet to make room for the most modern assembly line for the production of the Dino Fiat. However, the space where this line was once located is now taken up by the racing-car division, while the third side of the construction has been used for an aluminum foundry and services.

The number of personnel has kept increasing. In 1943 some 100 persons worked at the plant, a high percentage

Model 250 Europa

Model 410 Superamerica

Model 375 MM

Model 290 MM

Model 625 F1

Model 246 F1

Model 750 Monza

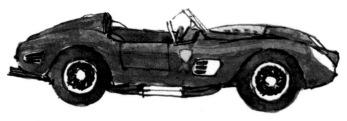

Model 250 TRS

of them women since the war was still on; by 1950 the number had doubled. In 1955 the total was some 250, and by 1961 it was 380. In these last ten years of expanding production the number of employees has reached 1,000.

Output of cars for the general public followed much the same pattern. We do not count the racing cars produced for an official squad of drivers: these have varied in number, never reaching more than 10 or 15 a year. The year 1947 marked the first sale of a Ferrari automobile. Seven were sold then with a climb to 45 in 1948. In 1949 sales were halted while retooling began for a new model. From 1950 to 1955, output averaged 70 to 80 cars a year; in the next five years there was a marked upswing, to over 300 cars in 1960; output climbed to 750 in 1965 and a high of 1,246 in 1971—all this without counting the final assembly of the Dino Fiat, which alone went far beyond the 1,000-a-year mark.

One factor easily overlooked by the layman, especially if he has not had the good fortune to visit the Maranello plant, is that the Ferrari cars have always been entirely built within the factory; this can find few comparisons in other automobile plants whether foreign or Italian. At the Ferrari plant every part used, from nuts to castings, from gears to chassis, is homemade, as it were. While this is no doubt because of a desire for secrecy of construction processes, it also arises from a realization that only the most meticulous control of the machine from beginning to end can guarantee the perfection that has made the Ferrari the most coveted of cars, even for collectors. And it was not by chance that owner clubs began to spring up, as was the case with the most illustrious makes of the past—the Bugatti, the Bentley, and so on.

Processing of the parts is handled by what might be called small-scale mass production, using the most detailed and costly means. For example, the crankshaft is cut from a cylindrical steel ingot by means of a series of processes involving lathework, milling, annealing, and so on, until at the end only one-sixth of the original piece of metal remains, and the finished, shining piece has acquired a beauty that rivals a work of modern art.

Where the processing becomes truly exceptional, and where it differs completely from the typical, big-industry assembly lines, is in the actual construction. Even with the agreement with Fiat, Ferrari officials refused to speed up production. It still remains largely that of the craftsman, with the individual worker dedicating himself to the assembly of a complete unit or section with all the time the job demands.

It's not surprising, then, that because of this deliberate precision work, and also because of the 1,000 employees more than 100 work in the racing-car and experimental section, the final product averages out to one car a year per employee.

In the case of a car already assigned to a buyer, the test-

Model 250 GT

Model 400 Superamerica

Model 156 F1

Model 246 P

Model 250 GTO

Model 250 LM

ing alone lasts days and days. First the finishing touches are put on the engine, then the suspension, the brakes, and all the rest are thoroughly tested. It has been wrongly claimed that Ferrari himself checks out all his cars. But it could be that when a test driver returns with a car ready for delivery he finds the big boss standing in the yard asking to go for a little ride. Then that particular car had better be in perfect condition. At least this was the situation before the contract with Fiat was signed; from that day the mass-production procedure came under the control of the Turin technicians, while Ferrari concerned himself only with the administration of his "stable."

As noted, the racing-car division of the Ferrari plant takes up one side of the main building, covering a space some eighty yards long and ten wide. Here the racing cars are built piece by piece, and then after each test dismantled for inspection. The processing of the individual parts is carried out in the mechanical section, and the engines are tested in the particularly well-equipped testing building, which has systems capable of handling speeds of more than 14,000 rpm and forces of more than 600 horsepower.

The work carried out by the mechanical division, always the most important part of the Ferrari plant, is without

doubt outstanding. You need only refer to the history of the sports car from 1946 (the year when the manufacturing of automobiles resumed at the Ferrari plant) to 1972 to discover a mass of production data, victories, and achievements that are probably without equal.

The Ferrari won the International Manufacturers Championship in 1952–54, 1956–58, 1960–64, 1967, and 1972 for 13 victories in 21 years. This left few championships for rivals like Mercedes, Aston Martin, Jaguar, Ford, and Porsche. The Ferrari plant built winning cars for five World Drivers Championships: 1952 and 1953 (Alberto Ascari), 1956 (Manuel Fangio), 1958 (Mike Hawthorn), 1961 (Phil Hill—the first time a United States driver won the title racing in Europe), and 1964 (John Surtees).

Competitors have increased in number and skill; drivers have challenged such traditional makes as Alfa Romeo, Maserati, Mercedes, and BRM by assembling their own racing cars, using parts from various sources (or "from the supermarket," as Ferrari puts it). The Lotus, the Brabham, the McLaren, and the Surtees are examples of this new look in that most highly competitive sports racing known as Formula 1. Other names such as Matra and March are worthy of the fullest respect. Often they have had technical and financial backing compared to

Model 330 GT 2 + 2

Model 500 Superfast

Model 158 F1

Model 275 GTS

which the Ferrari faded into the background. Even so the European Mountain Championship with special sports cars was won by the Ferrari in 1962 and 1965 with Scarfiotti and in 1969 with Peter Schetty; attempts were also made in Formula 2 competition at Indianapolis and elsewhere.

While all this work produced thousands of victories over a span of twenty-five years, it was at times counterproductive in the sense that, engaged simultaneously on so many fronts, Ferrari suddenly found himself short of time, men, and mechanical means to beat his rivals. It should not be forgotten that these rivals were serious and were tackling racing problems with ever more scientific procedures.

It can be said that Ferrari hesitated in adopting mechanical innovations (the rear-mounted engine); or that on the contrary he plunged into such advanced construction methods that valuable time was taken away from actual production; or that again trouble sprang from disagreements between the owner and this or that member of his staff. Failures might be caused by these, but not by a lack of tenacity or willingness to "try everything possible," as Enzo Ferrari himself, an honoris causa engineer, put it.

At Maranello, above the boss's office, there is a room

called "the chamber of horrors," a series of glass cases preserving all the parts which, by breaking down spectacularly during a race, hurt the Ferrari team. According to Ferrari these exhibits do not represent bad luck, for bad luck does not exist for him; the trouble was caused by things that certain persons could not or did not want to do.

In one corner of the grounds there is a small building set aside for racing or experimental cars that are no longer in use: after having been subjected to all possible tests and modifications, they end up in melancholy bits and pieces. Some cars are more fortunate than others, however, for they are saved intact and donated to museums. Across the street from the factory is the Dino Ferrari Professional Training School, which was created to train the highly specialized manpower that modern industry demands. The factory installations were completed with the building of a test track, a necessary luxury that the Ferrari of the hectic years before and after the war could not have permitted himself (there was not even a true "Ferrari" factory at this time), but that the Ferrari who was a "partner" of Fiat immediately ordered built. No question about it, when you're nearly seventy-three and decide to spend a billion lira on a test track, that's *real* enthusiasm.

21

The Garda course, 1950,
with a 125 F1 rolling
along.

24

A QUARTER OF A CENTURY OF IMPROVEMENTS

Through the intensity and continuity of his efforts, Ferrari has greatly contributed to the perfection of the engine of high-performance cars. The engineer Enzo Ferrari has always thought in terms of competition, and his contribution in this domain is undeniable. For him the production of great passenger cars has been an indispensable means of survival in an age that has been all too stingy in material rewards for the makers of sports and racing cars.

An automobile is not just an engine, and naturally great improvements have been made to the rest of the car, but there is no doubt that most of the attention goes to the engine. And it was in the design of new engines that the firm made its greatest investment.

Cars bearing the Cavallino emblem have distinguished themselves from the outset by their complex, refined 12-cylinder engine, which even today has found few imitators. The evolution of this type of engine in twenty-five years can be assessed with a few statistics. The first model in 1946 had a capacity of 1,500 cm^3, and developed 72 horsepower. The current 365 mass production model has a 4,400 cm^3 capacity and develops 350 horsepower, while externally it is no larger than the initial model. The 5-liter competition motor develops more than 600 horsepower.

Many technicians have taken turns in directing design, and this frequent change of the guard has made it possible to avoid technical stagnation while constantly gener-ating new ideas. It is hard to say whether or not the numerous changes have occasionally prejudiced results on the track, but the Ferrari has accumulated a valuable mass of data regarding its various experiments.

The first 12-cylinder motor was designed by the same Gioacchino Colombo who had already designed the Alfetta before the war and who in 1946 returned to the Ferrari firm, remaining until 1952. Early in 1948 he was joined by the engineer Aurelio Lampredi, one of the best designers in the recent history of the automobile. He came to Ferrari from aeronautics and brought new methods for resolving problems. During his stay, which lasted until 1955, he contributed to the build-ing of more powerful racing-car motors, like the fa-mous 4,500 cm^3 model for Formula 1, which beat the Alfa Romeo 158 several times and which could have won the World Championship had it not been for an incredible series of tire troubles. Another car of his design was the 500-type for Formula 2, one of the best racing cars of all time. Lampredi recalls designing the whole motor on one hectic Sunday when he worked uninterruptedly at the drawing table while Ferrari brought him sandwiches so that he could keep on with-out losing a minute.

When Lampredi left, the firm still had Alberto Massi-mino, who had arrived earlier that year and stayed on throughout 1956, along with the engineer Bellentani, who left in 1957. Bellentani was succeeded by the unfortunate engineer Fraschetti, who was killed in August 1957 while testing a new car at the Modena track.

The engineer Chiti then took over the post of head designer, leading Ferrari back to success with cars with the engine in the front; later, in the back. He dramatically reversed one of Ferrari's fundamental concepts: "The horses are always hitched in front." Chiti quickly regained the status lost to the British, but he left in 1962, to be replaced by newcomers like Forghieri, Rocchi, Bussi, Marelli, Caliri, and Ferrari (no relation).

Others besides designers made significant contributions: the ever-faithful Bazzi, a true wizard when it came to engines; the engineer Amorotti, who for years directed the racing team with passion; and a young Swiss technician, Michel May, who made great contributions to perfecting the fuel injection systems.

The first Ferrari had a capacity of 1,500 cm³ and was listed as a two-seater sports car called the 125-type in the catalog published at the end of 1946. The catalog also announced the young enterprise's manufacturing program by stressing three models, all with the same 12-cylinder engine, with the cylinders lined up in two rows of 6 each at a 60° angle. There was a touring car with a 72 horsepower, 5,400 rpm engine; a second more powerful model with 118 horsepower and 6,800 rpm; and, lastly, a one-seater for Formula 1 whose power was not yet known. In 1947 a number of sports cars were built and sold to sportsmen attracted by the unusual design of the engine, with its 12 cylinders, an overhead camshaft for each row of cylinders, use of a light alloy, and so on. These characteristics have been preserved up to today, along with improvements made possible by experience and more advanced techniques. For example, the camshaft chain drive has been applied even to racing cars since 1956; before then, the geared drive was believed essential. The first engine had a cylinder diameter of 55 mm and a 52.5-mm stroke, with a unitary capacity of some 125 cm³. This explains the model's markings, which are in line with a system used at the Ferrari plant for many years.

The unitary capacity was increased in 1948 to build a 2-liter engine, and the new type was called the 166 because that was the volume of a cylinder.

Model 166 was an important prototype not only because of the innumerable versions that were built— sport, touring, racing, with or without compressor—but because it led to a whole series of new models, obtained by leaving the 58.8-mm stroke unchanged and increasing the bore as needed.

In general, all Ferrari motors have had a stroke inferior to the bore, but there was one perfectly "square" motor with a diamter and stroke of 68 mm and a number of 4- and 6-cylinder motors built at the time of Lampredi which had a long stroke. These motors functioned perfectly and some of them scored outstanding successes.

Model 330 P2

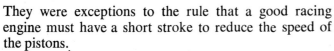

Model 206 Dino

They were exceptions to the rule that a good racing engine must have a short stroke to reduce the speed of the pistons.

In 1951 the regulations for Formula 1 established for one-seater cars demanded a maximum capacity of 1,500 cm³ with a compressor and 4,500 cm³ without compressor. At the Ferrari plant attempts were made with some success with supercharged motors, derived from the common block of the original 125. At first a one-stage compressor was mounted; then a two-stage one; finally an experiment was made with a three-stage supercharger aimed at outperforming the Alfa Romeo.

Nevertheless, in 1949 Lampredi suggested a possibility of obtaining better results with a compressorless engine, in view of the great advantage afforded by the 3 to 1 ratio in connection with the strict displacement set by the formula rules. From this came a series of big Ferrari engines with a 3,300 cm³ capacity prototype, called the 275, as usual because of its unitary capacity. It had a diameter of 72 mm and a 68-mm stroke; then the diameter was raised to 80 mm and the capacity to 4,100 cm³ (340 type); finally the stroke was raised to 74.5 mm and the capacity to 4,500 cm³ (375 type).

These engines and their successors represented a decisive turning point in motor technology. Not only did they beat racing rivals, but they proved it was possible to improve building techniques and specific performance.

To increase power, and at the same time keep weight to reasonable limits, the Ferrari people had to come up with new developments. Considering that in 1951 the 4,500-cm³ compressorless engine had 384 horsepower and weighed only 175 kilograms, the results can be considered highly successful. In order to combine less weight with great strength, a block engine was designed with thin but double walls about 2 centimeters apart, and this structure, though more complicated from the standpoint of fusion, had a particularly high degree of rigidity and resisted buckling. So there were no longer complaints of oil leaks or seized bearings. To obtain

great power, intake and exhaust manifolds were studied, using techniques which are common today but were a radical departure at the time.

A double ignition system was also used: two separate systems fed two spark plugs for each cylinder, to ensure a maximum efficiency of combustion.

The advantages obtained were obvious considering that the specific horsepower of this model, 85 horsepower per liter, was almost double that of the nonsupercharged engines of the period. One of the thorniest problems of high-speed engines—finding sufficiently resistant cylinder head gaskets—was neatly solved by screwing the cylinder barrels into the heads, eliminating gaskets altogether and leaving the barrels free to expand in the block.

The Formula 1 for 1,500–4,500-cm³ cars was to remain in effect until 1953, but interest in them had already declined in 1951, and people decided to focus attention on Formula 2 for one-seaters with compressorless engines and a capacity of only 2 liters. Within the limits of this formula, the first Ferrari engine with four cylinders in a row was built, the 500 type which Lampredi designed in just one day. This was followed by many other engines with 4 or 6 cylinders in a row, with double overhead camshafts and often with double ignition systems and two or three horizontal, twin-body carburetors, making it possible to feed each cylinder with independent pipe. Also characteristic of the in-line motor was the structure of the cylinder head, which continued downward to form the water chamber of the cooling system, with tightly screwed cylinder barrels, yielding pin-type valve springs, and, it goes without saying, dry crankcase lubrication.

From the 2-liter competition model of 1952 came 2.5-, 3-, and 3.5-liter models, with 4 and 6 cylinders. Leaving the dimensions of the 4-cylinder engine unchanged, but raising the number of cylinders to 6, the capacity was increased by half; by altering the bore or the stroke or both, the builders obtained the dimensions of the 625, 735, 750, and 860 in the sport and one-seater variant which was widely used until 1956–57.

The biggest engine with cylinders in line was built in

Model 312 B

Model 365 GTC 4

1956 for the car with which Nino Farina was to try his luck at Indianapolis. The vehicle had an American Kurtis Kraft frame and the motor was equipped with 6 cylinders in a row with a 102-mm bore and a stroke of 90 mm, which amounted to a total capacity of 4,412 cm³. This was numbered 446, standing for the 4,400 capacity and 6 cylinders, in accordance with a nomenclature that had been brought into use in 1955 to indicate certain models such as the 256 for Formula 1 (2,500 cm³ capacity and 6 cylinders) and the celebrated 252, a twin-cylinder 2½-liter type designed for tracks such as Monte Carlo, where a constant acceleration is demanded and thus an engine with high torque at low speed. Owing to difficulties in stability this engine failed to achieve its potential, but the experiment was interesting and useful. We have called attention to two systems used—often simultaneously—for naming the Ferrari models: unitary capacity, and a combination of the total capacity and number of cylinders. For some models, such as the 400 and 500 Superamerica and Superfast, a third system was brought into play, with the number merely indicating total capacity (4 or 5 liters) divided by 10.

The nomenclature of the Ferrari models is quite complicated, in that the markings made public are not the same as those used for identification purposes in the factory. Particularly with the models of the early years, one number was used to identify the engine (progressively increasing from 100, which was the first), a second to indicate the chassis, and a third public number for the finished car.

The V-shaped 12-cylinder engines and those with 4 and 6 cylinders in line were followed by ones with 6 cylinders in a V-shaped engine, better known as the Dino, after Ferrari's son who died young. The boy was already passionately devoted to his father's business and had taken the new and more compact engine to heart, writing to people about it and even publishing two articles on it in a magazine.

At first glance it would seem that a V6 is half of a V12, but this is not so. Problems stemming from balance and

space made it necessary to design the engine from scratch. The V6s of the Ferrari firm have usually been characterized by a 65° angle between the two rows of 3 cylinders. One type was built with a 120° angle.

Between 1956 and 1957, experiments were also made with engines with 8 cylinders arranged in a V at a 90° angle. This choice sprang from the altogether unexpected withdrawal of the Lancia from competition after the loss of its best driver, Alberto Ascari, and the gift of all its racing equipment to Ferrari. The designer of the one-seater Lancia was the engineer Jano, who now found himself back with his old friend. He now received the assignment of perfecting the Lancia model, whose unmistakable outline came from the external fuel tanks.

However, the V-shaped 8-cylinder type was never particularly popular at the Ferrari plant, and only a few versions were added to the original one of 2,500 cm³. There were a few variants for sports cars and a very brief return to competition in 1964 with a new 1,500-cm³ V8 for the then reigning Formula 1.

The 6-cylinder, on the other hand, had a highly active life. Created with a minimum capacity of 1,500 cm³ as a 156 type, it was later increased to 2 liters, then to 2.5 and 3 liters, and up to a maximum of 3,200 cm³ in 1958 for a car built to compete with the big American racing cars on the track at Monza.

At least twenty-five variations of the Dino engine, in various V-shaped versions, were built, if we count all the combinations of bores and strokes that were used, if only on an experimental basis.

Formula 2 models of the past few years were given heads with four valves to each of the 6 cylinders, a system already tested briefly on a 4-cylinder model, and shafts with the cams closer together. To save space it was necessary to abandon the twin ignition system and to return to a single spark plug per cylinder even for racing cars. This triggered a technical speedup in the field of ignition, which led the Marelli firm to build the capacitive discharge ignition Dinoplex system, which turned out to be better than all the others.

Though the last word in technical perfection, the Ferrari

The 1969 12 Hour
Sebring. Debut of
the Ferrari 312 P.

engines where rarely revolutionary. No Ferrari engine, for instance, has ever used desmodromic valve controls, and even the injection system, which was quickly adopted for racing cars, could not be called pioneering work.

However, an interesting job was done with the engine based on horizontal cylinders laid out in two opposite or boxer rows. The first model was built while the Formula 1 of 1,500 cm³ was on the way out in 1965, and was baptized at Monza by Bandini. This was the model 512, signifying 1,500 cm³ and 12 cylinders. The same number, with a new meaning of 5 liters (5,000 cm³) and 12 cylinders, was used for the sports cars of the seventies, no doubt further confusing those who have not been initiated into the peculiarities of Ferrari nomenclature.

In spite of the change in Formula 1, the boxer engine was not set aside, but served as a basis for a more powerful version with 2-liter capacity, used on the car with which Schetty won the Mountain Championship. This engine produced excellent results, in terms of power; perfect balance helped it to turn at high speed and to develop more than 300 horsepower, that is to say, a specific power of 150 horsepower per liter. As a consequence, another engine was built with flat or boxer cylinders, also for Formula 1, with 3-liter capacity. After a difficult developmental phase, this engine gave exceptional results, even outstripping the 2-liter models. Internal friction was reduced by using only four crankshaft bearings instead of the seven traditional ones, to produce an engine of extraordinary compactness. Measuring some 70 centimeters in length and breadth and 20 centimeters high, in 1970 it represented the apex of technology in the field of conventional piston engines, with more than 470 horsepower obtained from a weight of approximately 175 kilograms, without a compressor and burning ordinary gasoline.

Less spectacular progress has been made with the chassis. The chassis of the Ferrari sports models, like those of the single-seaters, at first consisted of two tubular side frame units joined by two transverse beams, with rigid front-wheel suspensions in parallelograms and a rigid back axle. The last-mentioned was used for a very long time in passenger cars, primarily because of great simplicity in manufacture compared to the more precise but more complex independent suspension.

On the other hand, racing cars always had independent rear-wheel suspension, or, in some cases, the De Dion rear axle as in the single-seaters of the fifties. Little by little the chassis evolved as well, with the main braces becoming thinner and, with the use of reinforcements, formed a sort of upper metal framework. In the end, with the models of the Lancia merger (called Lancia-Ferraris in fact), a full-fledged metal-framework chassis began to emerge, with the engine itself contributing a strengthening factor. From 1958 on, the chassis was a network of fairly good-sized piping, a system that was

Two views of the Ferrari "competition" division during car assembly.

never to be abandoned, though it has been partly modified lately by riveting plates on the various pipes of the framework, to strengthen the whole.

The two big changes in the chassis were the adoption of the disk brake and the shifting of the engine to the rear, both introduced rather late compared to some of Ferrari's competitors and only when it became urgent to do so.

It was relatively easy to modify the brakes or the suspension, but moving the engine to the rear was difficult. (It would be more accurate to say that the engine was shifted to a central position, since it is located forward of the rear axle or practically in the "center" of the chassis.) The position of the engine was a controversial question to Ferrari. In a memorable press conference he stated flatly that the only vehicles he knew of with engines in the center were buses. Not long afterward, though, circumstances made him build some of the fastest "buses" in the world—his racing cars of the sixties. Though these cars were often heavier and harder to drive than those of Ferrari's rivals, they were brutally powerful and fast. Ferrari, in fact, has never wanted to compromise even with himself on the safety factor and has never built fragile, short-lived cars.

Suspensions have undergone changes to match the evolution of the tire; research for the best possible solution to the problem never stopped. As Ferrari changed from the solid axle in back to swinging axles, and from these to the De Dion axle, superior road-holding capabilities came soon. Adoption of the independently sprung rear wheels of the 1960 one-seater, a forerunner of the new Formula 1 cars, was a milestone.

As the new formula progressed, with tire size tending to increase, suspensions remained the same except for refinements. Ferrari technicians have made important contributions here, with numerous innovations in the struts and the position of the strut sockets, particularly in connection with the rear wheels. Finally, in the 1971 single-seater, an experiment was made using a completely different system of rear-wheel suspension, with the spring-shock absorber groups of each wheel placed in a horizontal position above the differential box.

Ferrari was also the first to mount stabilizing ailerons on single seaters. They were at first fixed in place and then they were made electrically adjustable by the driver while racing.

Among experimental models that didn't get beyond the prototype stage was the small Mille, which the public got a look at thanks to photographs that were sneaked out and which was immediately christened the Ferrarina or baby Ferrari. It was a small high-performance sports car with a coupe body and an engine with 4 cylinders in a row with a capacity of 850 cm^3 and then 1,000 cm^3. It was tested from 1960 to 1961, but later abandoned. It served as a basis for a similar project of a short-lived Milan firm.

Another fascinating project was a one-seater racing car with a transverse air-cooled motor in the rear. This came out of a friendly meeting between Ferrari and the motorcycle manufacturer Gilera around 1961. But after the designs had been completed, it was never mentioned again.

Then there was that 1969–70 curiosity (because of its technical characteristics), the double-V engine, intended in design either to be a 12-cylinder short equivalent to an 8-cylinder (by making 4 rows of 3 cylinders each instead of the customary 2 lines of 6) or to capitalize on the outstanding 2-liter-engine cylinder and make a 3-liter engine with 18 cylinders arranged in three rows of 6 cylinders each.

Ever since the firm's connection with Firestone made it possible to count on drivers with expert knowledge of American tracks, such as Mario Andretti, and the association with Fiat greatly facilitated matters on the technical and financial level, Ferrari officials have been thinking about building a car capable of winning the one victory not written down in the golden book of the house—the Indianapolis 500.

Cars destined for this specialized American track can have either a free suction or supercharged engine and, taking no chances, Ferrari has built both versions, starting from the many existing motors in the long list of cylinder capacities.

Gianni Agnelli and Enzo Ferrari: a profitable collaboration between big-industry mass production and small-factory handicraft.

... AND THEN CAME FIAT

On June 21, 1969, a terse communiqué from the Fiat press office announced that the Turin automotive firm had entered into joint management of the Ferrari SEFAC. This long-expected announcement closed a drawn-out, complex affair that had intrigued the automobile world, not so much because of its purely commercial importance (the Citroën deal, signed at about the same time, was far more vital to Fiat), as for sentimental reasons.

Many times in the past, whenever some problem bothered Ferrari, he had threatened to shut down, to sell out, to move to another country. He insisted vehemently that nobody understood his problems. He made it clear that in Italy this lack of understanding came from the very people who had profited, if only indirectly, from his work in the sports-car field, which contributed to Italy's national prestige. Ferrari's leaving Italy appeared certain in 1964, when bargaining began with the Ford Motor Company for the sale of his company—actually, not so much outright sale as a sort of association. Enzo Ferrari would have had 90 percent of the sports-car management, giving the remaining 10 percent to Ford. The opposite would have held for the industrial side of the operations: 10 percent for Ferrari and 90 percent for Ford.

Ford technicians came to Maranello and began examining the plant in detail, evaluating its worth. After endless dickering and calculation, an agreement was reached on a figure that well-informed sources have put at $10 million. It was a worthwhile deal for Ford because, along with the value of the plant, which at that time had an annual output worth about half the cost figure, there was a tremendous accumulation of technical racing experience. In four years of competition Ford had spent far more than Ferrari's asking price.

At the last minute, as everyone knows, just when the preliminary agreement was ready for his signature, Ferrari suddenly backed down. Later he explained study of the various clauses, which were translated to him from the English text, showed that the contract would have stripped him of all power to make independent decisions. Ford officials were obliged to ask the consent of general management whenever a planned operation exceeded the amount budgeted.

However, one detail has remained unrevealed until now. One night in 1964 the author of this book had an accidental meeting with Pininfarina at the Turin railroad station. The great auto body maker, who was also vice-president of Ferrari SEFAC, was leaving for Modena. He said he was deeply worried over the way negotiations were going between Ford and Ferrari. He wanted to put Ferrari on his guard against the risks of binding himself hand and foot to the Americans. The worst risk would be the loss of his independence, and for a man like Ferrari this was crucial.

Pininfarina's arguments must have carried weight. They may also have included a promise of help from Fiat. In any case, not long afterward, in May 1965, engineer Piero Gobbato was sent from Fiat "on loan." This invaluable technician's function was to modernize the shop

in line with mass-production procedures. Gobbato remained at the Ferrari plant up to November 1966, but even before that Fiat already had a powerful figure close to Ferrari in the person of Francesco Bellicardi, director general of the Weber carburetor factory, a man who knew how to combine his gifts as a highly expert technician with great tact. Certainly in the numerous meetings between Ferrari and Bellicardi the discussion did not center around carburetors alone, but also on all the problems then plaguing the automobile manufacturer. Among these were the regulations just spelled out for Formula 2. The engine for the single-seater of this type could not have more than 6 cylinders and had to be derived from an ordinary assembly-line sedan of which at least five hundred had to be turned out annually. And the Ferrari plant could not hope to build five hundred 6-cylinder Dinos; its entire annual output of all models scarcely approached this figure.

Then on March 1, 1965, it was reported that Fiat would use the Ferrari Dino engine for a model of its own, of which several thousand would be built. The same engine could be used for the single-seater Formula 2 Ferrari. While this kind of help was just what Ferrari needed, it gave rise to all sorts of speculation. But in April, Fiat made it clear that it had not purchased the Ferrari plant. Only an agreement was involved, on the basis of which the Dino engine would be manufactured in Turin with the technical assistance of the Ferrari firm.

For Fiat it was a revolutionary development. To switch from a simple engine with a camshaft in the engine block to one with four camshafts above was one thing, but to agree to manufacture an engine designed and built outside the sacred precincts of the Mirafiori plant was earth-shaking. Some people wanted to change things in order to make the engine more suitable for mass production, while others didn't want to touch a nut or bolt of the shop favorite bearing the most treasured of all names. The Dino Fiat was first produced with 2-liter capacity, later reduced to 1,600 cm^3 in the Formula 2 version. Subsequently the capacity was raised to 2,400 cm^3, both for the Fiat version with the engine in front and for the Dino Ferrari model with the transversal engine in the rear.

The results were misleading, perhaps because the single-seater Ferrari took too long to be perfected. The author believes that the Dino engine could have been the national Italian engine of the years 1965–70 if it had been produced for sale to all manufacturers and outfitters of single-seaters. Instead these had to use the only engine available, a British one.

While the Dino program continued, the International Sporting Committee, the agency that directs automobile racing, decreed that to take part in the World Manufacturers Championship, manufacturers would have to choose between two alternatives, opting either for prototypes with 3-liter capacity engines, or for sports cars with 5-liter engines, on condition that at least twenty-five of the latter were manufactured. Deeply embittered, Ferrari at first gave up the idea of taking part in the races, feeling he was the victim of a plot. After all, only an entrepreneur in a particularly strong economic position could guarantee the manufacture of twenty-five cars, each of which cost more than $30,000, involving an outlay of not far from a million dollars—little of which could be expected to be offset by immediate sale of cars. Porsche was one of the first factories to comply with the new regulations, but Porsche turns out over 15,000 cars a year and enjoys a particularly solid financial position, owing to a high income from patents and from collabo-

ration with a number of the biggest automobile firms. Nevertheless, Ferrari changed his mind, and on April 24, 1969, just before the 1,000 Kilometer Monza race, he confided to the author that he too would manufacture the twenty-five cars required by the regulation in order to use 5-liter capacity. This was confirmed in an article in the April 30, 1969, edition of the Turin daily, *La Stampa,* which caused considerable excitement. It could only be inferred then that, unless he had won a large lottery or received an inheritance from some unlikely American uncle, Ferrari had the backing of the only Italian firm with the necessary means and interests in the automotive field. That would mean Fiat or, to be precise, its president, Gianni Agnelli.

Confirmation was not long in coming, and on June 21, 1969, Fiat announced that it had entered into the Ferrari business on a joint-management basis. This accord was much like what had been considered with Ford. It marked virtually the complete surrender of the mass production of Dino and Ferrari sedans to Fiat, while in the sports-car division, which was separate from the rest of the company and operated as an independent plant, Enzo Ferrari's authority remained unquestionable, even though, officially, he wanted to appear as no more than a consultant, alongside of Bellicardi, the deputy administrator. Naturally certain clauses in the agreement stipulate that some day Fiat will take over the Maranello plant completely.

So, fifty years after that dramatic episode on the bench in Valentino Park, an end has come to a historic cycle in Italian automobile manufacturing, one that saw many individuals follow one another from Turin to Milan, from Milan to Maranello, and finally back to Turin, the cradle of Italian motoring.

Indissolubly tied to one of the greatest automobile complexes in the world, the Ferrari name has assured itself a long life, though purists are convinced that the Ferraris produced after 1969 can never be the equal of those turned out when the firm was on its own.

And yet since the merger with Fiat, quality has not slacked off; if anything the reverse is true. The technological processes and laboratory tests used are so complex and costly that only the biggest industrial complexes can afford them. Take for example the vast field of safety tests, or of control of exhaust fumes. Such fields demand particularly expensive installations and even the destruction of automobiles in perfect condition. It wrings the heart to think that so many Ferraris have been sent crashing into steel barriers just to test their resistance. But that's the way it is today. At Maranello, more and more cars with Turin license plates are to be seen in the parking lot of the Cavallino restaurant, while the plant itself is being enlarged and increasingly automated. Even the racing division has changed. The cars are still built by hand with painstaking care, but when a part breaks down in a race it is no longer placed in a glass case in the "chamber of horrors," but sent to Turin to be analyzed in laboratories and tested by computers. Even the "wizard of Maranello," as Ferrari has sometimes been called, has bought himself a computer.

PART TWO

PRODUCTION

125 S

Above left, the dashboard of the Ferrari 125/166; right, the same car preserved by an American museum in Long Island; below, the starting line at the 1948 Posilippo course in Naples.

In Italy, the wounds of the war were still open. Victor Emmanuel had abdicated in favor of his son Humbert, but there was a referendum and the nation voted for the republic. Humbert II quit Italy and De Nicola became the first head of the republic. This was 1946 and at the Ferrari plant, under the direction of designer Gioacchino Colombo, work had just been completed on the 125 S, a 1,500-cm³ car with aggressive lines, a large "snoot," and two seats backed up against the tail section.

The first Ferrari made its debut on May 5, 1947, at Piacenza, driven by Franco Cortese. It had to drop out of competition because of a fuel pump failure. This marked the first racetrack appearance of a car built entirely by the Ferrari plant.

The first success came some time later in the Grand Prix of Rome, which Cortese won at an average of 88 kilometers per hour (about 55 miles per hour). The same driver was at the wheel of the 125 S at Vigevano and Varese. The next to climb into a Ferrari was Tazio Nuvolari, one of the greatest drivers in the history of racing, who was about to retire. At the Forli track success was inevitable. The brief racing career of the 125 S in racing ended at Parma.

While the election of the first Miss Italy in Stresa on August 16 touched off a new form of mass enthusiasm, Franco Cortese won a race with the new 159 (the 125 S with a 1,900-cm³ engine) on the Pescara track, on August 16. On October 12 the same car, driven by Raymond Sommer, son of a rich farmer of the Ardennes, came in first at the Grand Prix of Turin, at an average speed of 108 kph.

The Ferrari plant turned out seven 125 Ss: three were

entrusted to official drivers and the others sold to private citizens. The engine was truly outstanding; the chassis was extremely simple—tubular with independent front wheels and rigid rear axles. The competition cars had spider-type bodies. Some had motorcycle-type fenders separated from the body. The engine, which at first was 1,500 cm³, was soon raised to 1,900 cm³ and was mounted on vehicles that had already been produced. A new engine, destined to propel the 125 GT, remained in the designing stage.

125 S

TECHNICAL SPECIFICATIONS

Engine: 4-stroke, front; 12 cylinders in V on 60° angle; bore and stroke, 55 × 52.5 mm; capacity, 1,496.7 cm^3; compression ratio, 9; maximum power output, 118 hp at 7,000 rpm; cylinder block and crankcase in single piece of light alloy, with barrels of special cast iron; cylinder head of light alloy, with hemispherical combustion chambers; 7-bearing crankshaft; side-by-side connecting rods; 2 valves per cylinder, actuated by 1 overhead camshaft per row of cylinders, with cam followers; camshaft powered by silent chain; distribution diagram, 15° 54° 54° 15°; fuel supply 3 inverted twin Weber carburetors, 30 DCF type; coil ignition with 2 distributors for 6 cylinders each; pressure lubrication, with oil radiator; water cooling system with pump, without fan; dynamo driven by the timing chain.

Drive: through rear wheels; single dry plate clutch and elastic hub; gearbox in unit with engine; 5 speeds + reverse, II, III, and V silent; shift ratio I, 3.09; II, 2.22; III, 1.38; IV; 1; V, 0.92; reverse, 3.95; axle ratio, 4.90.

Chassis: tubular side frames of elliptic section including tubular transverse beams; front wheels independent suspension, with upper and lower wishbones, lower transverse spring, and oleodynamic shock absorbers with rigid, semifloating axle, longitudinal springs, transverse stabilizing bar, and double-effect hydraulic shock absorbers.

Steering: parallel arms linkage, worm screw and sector.

Brakes: drums, with hydraulic control; hand brake on rear wheels.

Electrical equipment: 12-volt; generator.

Dimensions and weights: wheelbase, 2,420 mm; front track, 1,255 mm; rear track, 1,200 mm; weight of complete car chassis, 570 kg; weight of vehicle, 750 kg; tires, 5.50 × 15; fuel tank capacity, 75 liters.

Performance: maximum speed in I, 46 kph; II, 64 kph; III, 103 kph; IV, 142 kph; V, 153 kph.

The first Ferrari Sport taking a high-speed turn at the Piacenza course, Franco Cortese driving, at its debut (May 5, 1947).

The 166 S engine, which appeared in 1948, preserved the original structure and numerous details of the 159 type. It was the same engine that had been designed by Colombo and modified by Aurelio Lampredi. Arriving at the Ferrari plant early in 1948, Lampredi was to leave his imprint on the Ferrari output from 1948 to 1955.

The 166 S engine was initially mounted on a 125 S-type chassis, then made on a shorter chassis (wheelbase of 224 cm compared to 242 cm) which later on was to have carried other engines. The new type was called Mille Miglia (Thousand Miles) or MM.

In addition to the 166 S and MM types, the technicians brought out the Inter, which being designed for passenger cars was less powerful. The 166 engine was also used on the F2 single-seater (capacity limit 2,000 cm³ without compressor). One version was equipped with a Roots-type compressor mounted on a Formula 1 chassis. This hybrid was intended for open formula competi-

Left, the single-seater Formula 2 derived from the Sport by modifying the body work; above, the Ferrari 166 S of Sterzi and Righetti on the Lake Garda circuit, 1948; below, a Ferrari 166, nicknamed "little boat," on a difficult stretch in the Mille Miglia.

tions. The 195 type, with 2,340 cm³ capacity, evolved from the 166, but was soon given up.

As these engines were used in 1948–50, the most sensational story had to do with a 195 engine mounted on a 166-type car. The 1950 Mille Miglia was won by Giannino Marzotto, one of the four sons of the owner of the Valdagno wool mills, who teamed in the competition with Crosara. People were skeptical of him at the starting line when he arrived dressed in a conventional gray suit as if for a business luncheon. Covering the 1,682 kilometers at an average speed of more than 123 kph in his Ferrari, Giannino upset all the forecasts. The marathon went on record as the "Gray Suit Mille Miglia."

The success of the gentleman from Valdagno was only one of the many Ferrari wins in 1948–50. The machines from Maranello were given to the best drivers of the time. Clemente Biondetti won the Mille Miglia in 1948 and 1949 in a 166-type Ferrari. The Chinetti-Seldson team scored a prestigious win in a Ferrari at Le Mans in the first 24 Hour race of the postwar period, and Giovanni Bracco made a name in the climbing competitions.

The Ferraris driven by Chico Landi, Raymond Sommer, Alberto Ascari, and Gigi Villoresi succeeded almost everywhere. The "Rearing Pony" began to harvest the fruit of high-level construction techniques that put the red machines of Maranello well ahead of the competition.

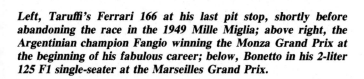

Left, Taruffi's Ferrari 166 at his last pit stop, shortly before abandoning the race in the 1949 Mille Miglia; above right, the Argentinian champion Fangio winning the Monza Grand Prix at the beginning of his fabulous career; below, Bonetto in his 2-liter 125 F1 single-seater at the Marseilles Grand Prix.

TECHNICAL SPECIFICATIONS

Engine: 4-stroke, front; 12 cylinders in V on 60° angle; bore and stroke, 60 × 58.8 mm; capacity, 1,995 cm^3; compression ratio, 8.5; maximum power output, 150 hp at 7,000 rpm; building characteristics and phasing of distribution as in 125 S type; fuel supply 3 inverted twin Weber carburetors, 30 DCF type and mechanical fuel pump; coil ignition with 2 distributors for 6 cylinders each; pressure lubrication, through oil radiator; water cooling system with pump driven by the timing chain, without fan.

Drive: through rear wheels; single dry plate clutch and elastic hub; gearbox in unit with engine; 5 speeds + reverse, II, III, and V silent gears; various axle ratios according to type of use.

Chassis: tubular side frames of elliptic section including transverse beams; front wheels independent suspension, with upper and lower wishbones, lower transverse spring, and Houdaille hydraulic shock absorbers; rear suspension with solid axle, longitudinal springs, and Houdaille hydraulic shock absorbers.

Steering: worm screw and sector.

Brakes: drum, hydraulic; hand brake on rear wheels.

Electrical equipment: 12-volt.

Dimensions and weights: wheelbase, 2,420 mm; front track, 1,255 mm; rear track, 1,200 mm; weight of vehicle, 800 kg; tires, 5.50 × 15; fuel tank capacity, 70 liters.

Performance: maximum speed, 190 kph.

Fuel: ternary mixture with high octane content, made up of gasoline, benzol, and ethyl alcohol, in more or less equal parts or with a preponderance of gasoline.

Ferraboschi

125 F1

Naturally Ferrari planned a single-seater racing car. Achieved in 1948, it carried the marking 125 F1, and the engine was equipped with a one-stage supercharger. In 1949 a new one-seater was prepared with a two-stage supercharger which considerably increased power.

In its two-year career, the 125 F1 underwent important modifications: the rear suspension with independent wheels and swinging drive shafts was replaced by a rigid De Dion axle to increase roadability. Straight roller bearings were used for the crankshaft bearings and double overhead camshafts took the place of the single camshaft used in 1948.

These single-seaters, which took the Ferrari name to track after track, turned out to be slower than the 8-cylinder Alfa Romeo 158, which, oddly enough, was conceived by Enzo Ferrari when he was working for the Milan firm. So began an all-out rivalry between Ferrari and Alfa Romeo, one that Ferrari finally won with no little effort.

The inferiority of the 125 to the 158 justified its withdrawal from competition. Its place was soon taken by the compressorless 4,500 and by the new single-seater with a 2-liter engine, which was entered in the World Drivers Championship run by Formula 2 cars in 1952–53.

After the resumption of great sporting events interrupted by the war, there was much talk of creating a

Alberto Ascari in his Ferrari 125 at the Grand Prix of Switzerland, 1949.

Two views of the Ferrari 166 restored to perfection as a valuable museum piece. This was the last 12-cylinder Formula 2 model; it was succeeded by a 4-cylinder model.

Above, the first Ferrari 125 F1; below, an improved model driven by Nino Farina; right, the last model of the car, with Alberto Ascari driving.

Formula 1 World Championship. Meanwhile the Ferraris were piling up victories in duels with Alfa Romeos, Maseratis, Delahayes, and Talbots. Nino Farina won the Garda circuit: the first victory for the 125 one-seater. (Interestingly enough, Farina was the nephew of body maker Pininfarina, who was to play an important role in the Ferrari firm's commercial successes, also contributing to the racing division with his body work and aerodynamic studies.)

Alberto Ascari won the Grand Prix of Switzerland at Bern at an average of over 146 kph; Gigi Villoresi won at Zandvoort, Holland; then it was Ascari's turn in England, on the Silverstone circuit. Peter Whitehead ended the season with a win at Brno, Czechoslovakia.

Ferrari then gave up the supercharged 1,500, but the cars were then taken over by such independents as Chico Landi, who scored numerous victories with them in Brazil.

125 F1

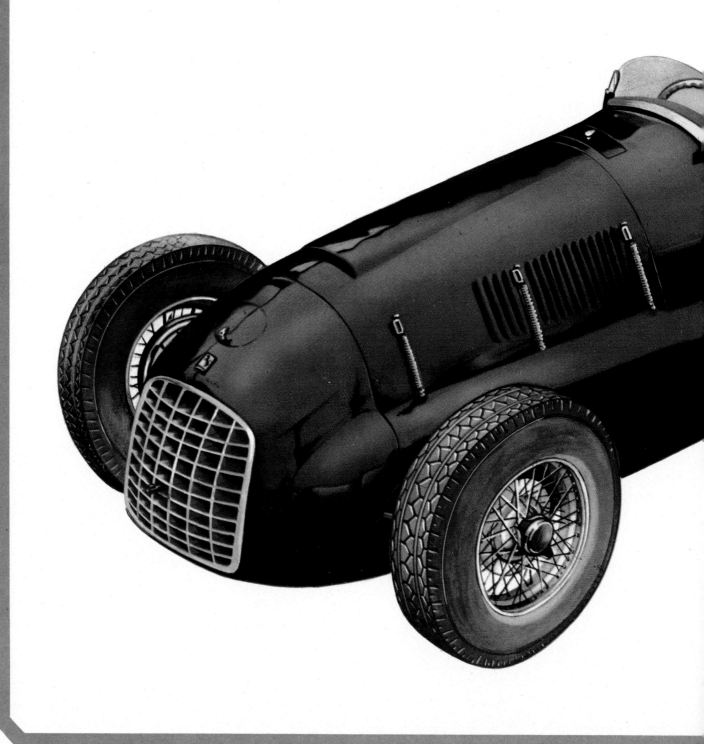

Ferraboschi

TECHNICAL SPECIFICATIONS

Engine: 4-stroke, front; 12 cylinders in V on 60° angle; bore and stroke, 55 × 52.5 mm; capacity, 1,496.7 cm³; compression ratio, 6.5; boost of supercharger, 1.1 atmospheres; maximum power, 230 hp at 7,000 rpm; building characteristics common to other models; 2 valves per cylinder operated by 1 overhead camshaft for each row of cylinders with cam followers; diagram of distribution, 18° 58° 54° 22°; fuel supply 1 triple Weber carburetor, 50 WCF type; twin magneto ignition, each for row of 6 cylinders powered by rear end of camshaft; pressure lubrication with dry crankcase radiator; water cooling system.

Chassis: tubular side frames of elliptic section including transverse beams; front wheels independent suspension, with upper and lower wishbones, lower transverse spring, and Houdaille shock absorbers; rear suspensions with independent wheels, swinging axles, stress braces, lower transverse spring, and Houdaille shock absorber.

Steering: worm screw and sector.

Brakes: drums on 4 wheels, with hydraulic circuit separate for front and rear wheels.

Dimensions and weights: wheelbase, 2,160 mm; front track, 1,270 mm; rear track, 1,250 mm; weight of vehicle, 700 kg; front tires, 5.50 × 15; rear tires, 6.50 × 16; fuel tank capacity, 120 liters.

Performance: maximum speed, 240 kph.

Fuel: mixture based on methyl alcohol, 80%; ethyl alcohol, 10%; benzol, 5%; acetone, 2%; petroleum either, 2%; castor oil, 1%.

⌖ 212 EXPORT

The 12-cylinder 125-type Ferrari engine has been stepped up in capacity, from 125 to 159, then 166, then 195, and then 212. This rise seemed to have no end with progressive increases in the bore (though the stroke remained at 58.8 mm) production achieved a 225 type, then a 250, and finally the 275.

This increase was dictated by the need to equip the first cars for a clientele not exclusively devoted to the sports world. The racing Ferrari had attracted a very special public of famous names in art and high society.

So the limited commercial program began with the manufacture of the 195 Inter, which used a less powerful version of the engine of the 1950 Mille Miglia car. Production then turned to the 212 Export and then the Inter chassis (long wheelbase, less powerful engine) and Export (short chassis, racing competition engine) received the 212 engine. The spider versions also carried the 225 type. Production of the 212 continued until 1953, and the bodies were signed by such celebrated names as Vignale, Ghia, and Touring. The 212 signaled an important collaboration between Ferrari and Pininfarina. The first Ferrari with a body by Pinin was the 212 Inter cabriolet in 1952.

The Ferraris continued to win. These were the great years of the gentlemen drivers, willing to spend millions of lire to be allowed to drive a thunderous racing car. The Marzotto brothers drove Ferraris to new victories: Vittorio in the Tour of Sicily and the Grand Prix de Monaco reserved (in 1952) for racing cars; Giannino in the Tuscany Cup; Paolo in the Dolomite Gold Cup, the Senigallia circuit, and the Tour of Calabria. Besides

the offspring of the "wool king," some of the greats in the world of racing were Gigi Villoresi, who in winning the third Inter-Europe Cup at Monza suggested the name to be given the small sedan; the Taruffi-Chinetti and Ascari-Villoresi teams, who dominated the grueling Carrera Panamericana of more than 3,000 kilometers; Biondetti, Scotti, Cornacchia, Sterzi, Toselli, who were linked to the Ferrari 195, 212, and 225 models and their derivatives. Chinetti in particular was often involved in the history of the Ferrari firm, not so much as a driver but as distributor for the Ferrari in North America. A sports enthusiast, he created the North American Racing Team, which was to give the Ferrari make many wins.

Left, the Vignale fastback on a 212 Inter chassis; above, the historic first production model of the Ferrari-Pininfarina 1952 cabriolet on a 212 Inter chassis; right, instrument panel of the Vignale spider.

212 EXPORT

TECHNICAL SPECIFICATIONS

Engine: 4-stroke, front; 12 cylinders in V at 60° angle; bore and stroke, 68 × 58.8 mm; capacity, 2,562.6 cm³; compression ratio, 7.5; maximum power, 150 hp at 6,500 rpm; building characteristics like preceding models; fuel supply 2 self-regulating mechanical pumps and 1 inverted twin Weber carburetor, 36 DCF type; coil ignition with 2 distributors for 6 cylinders each; pressure lubrication with 8 liters of oil in the crankcase; water cooling system with pump driven by the timing chain.

Drive: through rear wheels; single plate dry clutch with elastic hub; gearbox in unit with engine; 5 speeds + re

Ferraboschi

verse, II, III, and V silent; gear ratio I, 2.41; II, 1.74; III, 1.27; IV, 1; V, 0.92; axle ratio, 5 or 4.66.

Chassis: tubular side frames of elliptic section including transverse beams; front wheels independent suspension, with upper and lower wishbones, lower transverse spring, and Houdaille shock absorber; rear suspensions with double semielliptic springs for each wheel, rigid axle and Houdaille shock absorber.

Steering: worm screw and sector.

Brakes: drum, hydraulic, on 4 wheels; hand brake on rear wheels.

Dimensions and weights: wheelbase, 2,600 mm; front track, 1,278 mm; rear track, 1,250 mm; spoke wheels with rims in light alloy for 6.40 × 15 tires; weight of vehicle, 1,000 kg; fuel tank capacity, 105 liters.

Performance: maximum speed (at 6,500 rpm in the various gears with axle ratio 5): I, 70 kph; II, 97.5 kph; (with axle ratio 4.66): I, 75.5 kph; II, 104.5 kph; III, 143 kph; IV, 182 kph; V, 196.5 kph.

375 F1

Automobile racing has always been first in Enzo Ferrari's life. His desire to defeat Alfa Romeo remained keen, but he felt there was little hope of doing this with supercharged engines. He had full confidence in Lampredi, who had repeatedly stated that he could design and build a normally aspirated engine equal to or even superior to a supercharger. So

Left, Froilan Gonzales, "El Cabezon," winner of the Grand Prix of England at Silverstone in 1951 in a Ferrari 375 F1; above, the car built for the French champion Rosier—practically the first model based on the 4,500-cm³ single-seater.

TECHNICAL SPECIFICATIONS

Engine: 4-stroke, front; 12 in V at 60°; bore and stroke, 80 × 74.5 mm; capacity, 4,493 cm³; compression ratio, 11; maximum power, 350 hp at 7,000 rpm; cylinder block and heads of silumin, with barrels screwed in; 1 overhead camshaft per line of 6 cylinders; 60° angle between valves, cam followers, pin-type valve springs; valve timing, 24° 68° 70° 20°; fuel supply 2 pumps and 3 inverted twin Weber carburetors, 42 DCF type; dry crankcase lubrication; water cooling system.

Drive: through rear wheels; mutiple disk clutch; rear gearbox in unit with differential; 4 speeds + reverse; gearbox and axle ratio vary according to use.

Chassis: side frames and tubular tranverse beams; front wheels independent suspension, with upper and lower wishbones, lower transverse spring, and Houdaille shock absorbers; rear suspension with independent wheels, swinging axles, and transverse spring; both suspensions are integrated by special rubber stoppers which go into operation beyond a fixed deflection, modifying the elasticity of the suspension.

Brakes: hydraulic, drum, on 4 wheels, with 2 operating cylinders per wheel to ensure perfect adherence of shoes on bimetallic drums.

Dimensions and weights: wheelbase, 2,320 mm; front track, 1,270 mm; rear track, 1,250 mm; spoke wheels with light alloy rims for front tires of 5.50 × 16 and rear tires of 7.00 × 17; weight of complete engine, 195 kg; weight of car, 710 kg; fuel tank capacity, 195 liters.

Performance: maximum speed, with highest ratio, approximately 300 kph.

Fuel: mixture of gasoline, benzol, and alcohol.

Ferraboschi

they set existing chassis and engines aside and started anew. The 12V, 60° engine was redesigned with a greater distance between the cylinders, and a double-walled crankcase was added to make it lighter. Cylinder barrels were screwed into the heads to avoid gas leakages where the head and cylinder block were joined. The valve controls were equipped with rollers on the followers to reduce friction, and accurate measurements were made of the gas passages in the head, to enhance volumetric performance.

Though the engine got the most attention, the chassis and the drum brakes also received careful evaluation.

The engine, originally 3,300 cm³, was raised to 4,100 cm³ and then to 4,500 cm³. The, 3,300-cm³ engine was used experimentally in one of the cars in the 1950 Mille Miglia, and at last Enzo Ferrari could cry victory. The Alfa Romeos had arrived at the end of their cycle and often proved inferior to the Ferrari 4,500. In 1951, successes came in bunches, though the World Championship title was still held by Alfa Romeo with its exceptional driver Manuel Fangio, who won the first of his five titles that year. Even so, Ferrari drivers included Villoresi at Syracuse, Sicily, in the season opener and at Pau; Parnell at Silverstone and Goodwood; Gonzales at Silverstone and Pescara; and Ascari at the Nürburgring and Monza.

For Enzo Ferrari, the most important victory was the one scored at Silverstone by the big Argentinian Froilan Gonzales: it was the first head-to-head success of the 4,500 against the Alfa. Ferrari admitted that the news of the victory brought him both joy and pain, since the years he had spent at Alfa could not be wiped away just like that.

The 4,500-cm³ model left lasting memories at Ferrari because it was entered in the 1952 Indianapolis 500 with Ascari at the wheel. The big car was right up with the leaders when Ascari had to drop out with a broken wheel.

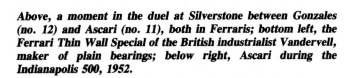

Above, a moment in the duel at Silverstone between Gonzales (no. 12) and Ascari (no. 11), both in Ferraris; bottom left, the Ferrari Thin Wall Special of the British industrialist Vandervell, maker of plain bearings; below right, Ascari during the Indianapolis 500, 1952.

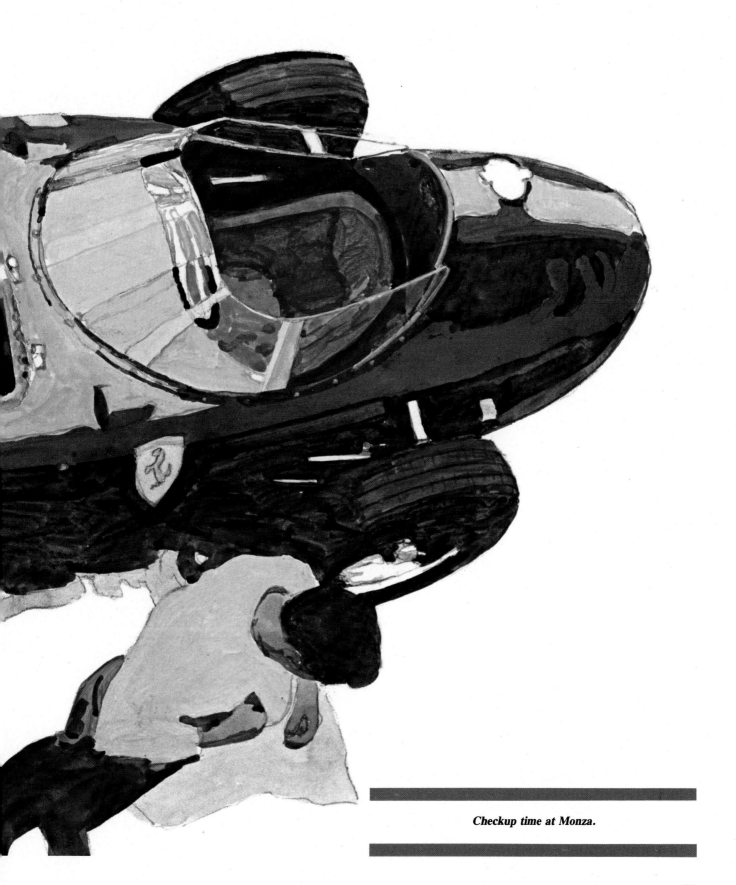

Checkup time at Monza.

◈ 500 F2

I n one day of uninterrupted concentration, designer Aurelio Lampredi worked out the broad outlines of the new Ferrari 500-type engine, a milestone in the history of the firm. It was a 4-cylinder model modified to replace the now traditional 12-cylinder model.

The 4 cylinders in line with twin overhead camshafts was first mounted in sports cars in the original version, then in a higher-powered model. The shift from 12 to 4 cylinders was prompted by the need to obtain a higher if less uniform torque. Lampredi's technique, already amply tested with the 4,500-cm³ model, was effective with the 2-liter engine. The engine used on the Formula 2 single-seater, along with the chassis, the result of solutions already widely tested (such as the rigid De Dion axle), proved its worth from the start.

The exceptional capabilities of the car were thoroughly exploited by Alberto Ascari, who won the world title in 1952 and 1953. The Italian champion won on all circuits in those two years, coming in first in 1952 at Syracuse and in Holland, Belgium, France, England, and West Germany (where, having scored his third straight success, he was proclaimed Nürburgringmeister)—and in Italy. In 1953 he won in Holland, Belgium, England, Argentina, and Switzerland.

For Italian sportsmen, 1953 was a year studded with triumphs, since the Ferrari's successes with Ascari, Hawthorn, Farina, and Pinto were matched by the victories of the Maserati with Fangio and de Graffenried.

Alberto Ascari, World Drivers Champion 1952–53, driving the amazing 500 F2 single-seater in which he won many victories.

Ferraboschi

TECHNICAL SPECIFICATIONS

Engine: 4-stroke, front; 4 cylinders in line; bore and stroke, 90 × 78 mm; capacity, 1,984.9 cm³; compression ratio, 12; maximum power, 170 hp at 7,000 rpm; cylinder block and crankcase of light alloy; cylinder head prolonged down to middle of stroke, with barrels screwed in and hemispherical combustion chambers; 5-bearing crankshaft; shaft completely counterbalanced; 2 valves per cylinder inclined at 85° angle; valves actuated by 2 overhead camshafts; through roller cam followers and driven by train of cylindrical gears; distribution diagram, 50° 80° 78° 48°; fuel supply through 2 horizontal twin Weber carburetors, 50 DCO type; twin ignition system with two magnetos powered by front gear train; dry crankcase lubrication; water cooling.

Drive: through rear wheels; multiple disk clutch; rear gearbox in unit with self-locking differential; 4 forward speeds + reverse; gearbox-differential ratio varies according to type of circuit.

Chassis: 2 tubular side frames with crossbeams; front wheels independent suspension, with upper and lower wishbones, lower transverse spring, rubber plugs, and Houdaille shock absorbers; rear suspension with rigid De Dion axle and transverse leaf spring.

Steering: parallel arms linkage and 3-section column, with universal joints for getting around engine.

Brakes: drum, hydraulic, on 4 wheels; diameter of drums, 350 mm; width of shoes, 48 mm.

Dimensions and weights: wheelbase, 2,160 mm; front track, 1,270 mm; rear track, 1,250 mm; front tires, 5.25 × 16; rear tires, 5.50 × 16; weight of car, 560 kg; fuel tank capacity, 150 liters.

Left, Ascari in the 1952 German Grand Prix; below, Bordeaux Grand Prix of 1953, two Ferrari 500 F2s, Villoresi in the first, with Ascari right behind him; above right, standing next to the car, Amorotti, director of the racing division, and Lampredi, engineer for Ferrari.

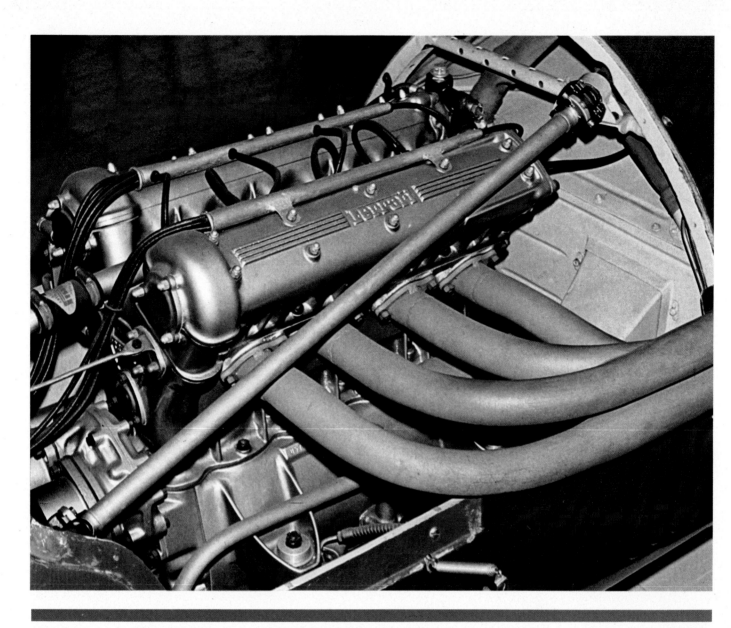

Above, the new 4-cylinder-in-a-line motor of the 500 F2, created in a single day by Lampredi; below left, the model displayed at Turin's Biscaretti Automobile Museum; top to bottom, right, the front and rear suspension which were the secret of the 500 F2's roadholding qualities; far right, the cockpit.

340 S

Naturally, the engines that had proved themselves in Formula 1 racing were used in sport and production models. While the 275 engine had little success in the 1950 Mille Miglia, the 340 type—4,101 cm³—found favor in such models as the 340 S, 340 Mexico, and 340 America (which later became the 342 America).

The 340 S, which added the letters MM after Giannino Marzotto's victory in the 1953 Mille Miglia, was perhaps the most widely sold type in all its versions. Bodies for these cars were built by Touring, which followed the lines of the well-known "barchetta" (little boat) 166 type. This was a spider, also called a Mexico type because it was especially designed for the Carrera Panamericana, though this grueling marathon was usually won by more powerful cars.

In all its versions, the 340 engine remained essentially unchanged, though its performance increased as the models moved from the normal passenger sedan type to the more high-powered. The small coupés, the work of Vignale, were produced in 1952–53. The chassis kept the same characteristics but varied in wheelbase—260 cm for the small coupés, 250 cm for the spiders.

The 340 series cars were planned for long, grueling endurance competitions or for brief hill races, proving that the Ferraris were equal to all contests. In 1952, the American Kimberly-Lewis team won the 12 Hour Vero Beach race, and Scotti won the timed hill climbs at Catania-Etna and Vermicino-Rocca di Papa. The car had its most spectacular success in 1953 when the Giannino Marzotto-Crosara team repeated their 1950 success in the Mille Miglia. This time Marzotto was a favorite, and his win confirmed the superiority of the Ferraris. The car, a spider type, averaged 142 kph. The same year, the red Ferraris scored other important successes with Hawthorn at Silverstone and with Pagnibon at Algiers and Paris.

Above right, Marzotto at the starting line of the Vermicino-Rocca di Papa, 1950; below right, Giovanni Bracco at the start of the 1952 Targa Florio in a Ferrari 340, spider version.

340 S

TECHNICAL SPECIFICATIONS

Engine: 4-stroke, front; 12 cylinders in V at 60° angle; bore and stroke, 80 × 68 mm; capacity, 4,101.6 cm³; compression ratio, 8; maximum power, 280 hp at 6,600 rpm; cylinder block and crankcase of light alloy, with twin hemispherical combustion chambers; 7-bearing crankshaft; connecting rods side by side; 2 valves per cylinder, actuated by 1 overhead camshaft per row of 6 cylinders; valve timing, 24° 68° 70° 20°; fuel supply, 3 inverted twin Weber carburetors, 40 DCF type; coil ignition with 2 distributors; pressure lubrication, with automatic pump; water cooling system.

Drive: through rear wheels; multiple metallic disk clutch; gearbox in unit with engine; 5 forward speeds + reverse, II, III, IV, and V silent; gearbox ratio I, 3.16; II, 1.95; III, 1.40; IV, 1; V, 0.91; axle ratio varies according to use.

Chassis: Steel tubular side frames with elliptic section; front wheels independent suspension, with upper and lower wishbones, single transverse spring, and Houdaille shock absorbers; rear suspensions with solid axle and 4 guide struts, longitudinal springs, and Houdaille shock absorbers.

Steering: parallel linkage, screw and helicoidal sector.

Brakes: drum on 4 wheels, with separate hydraulic circuits for front and rear wheels.

Dimensions and weights: wheelbase, 2,500 mm; front track, 1,325 mm; rear track, 1,320 mm; front tires, 6.00 × 16; rear tires, 6.50 × 16; weight of car, 850 kg; fuel tank capacity, 150 liters.

Fuel: high-test gasoline.

Ferraboschi

When Enzo Ferrari decided to conquer America with his prestigious cars, he knew he would have to come up with a model suitable for that market. He needed a car with a very powerful engine, and he immediately thought of the Formula 1 engine. The result was the 342 America, which developed 220–230 horsepower at 6,000 rpm. In a later version the power was cut down to 200 horsepower at 5,000 rpm to make the steering smoother. The Americans demanded an altogether different kind of car from the nervous, peppy little sedans so popular in Europe. The 190 kph (about 120 mph) of the 342 America was more than enough for the Americans.

The car answered the needs of motorists in the U.S. and continued to be produced even in 1953 in the 375 version. In 1955 it gave rise to a new car, the 410 Superamerica.

The Pininfarina firm built the bodies for all the versions of the America, giving the car lines of great luxury and enhancing it with all the extras available at the time.

The specter of the war was only an ugly memory now and people were again thinking of luxury and beautiful things. Owning a Ferrari became a success symbol; for the Americans it was visible evidence of having it made. These cars were not bought only by the Americans. Their celebrated owners included the Aga Khan, Ingrid Bergman, the royal family of Belgium, and Gianni Agnelli.

Above left, the 2 + 2 coupe, type 342 America (later equipped with the 375 motor), with body by Pininfarina as usual; below left, the two-seater coupe with the characteristic swept-back rear; below, the two-seater cabriolet on a 375 America chassis.

TECHNICAL SPECIFICATIONS

Engine: 4-stroke, front; 12 cylinders in a V at a 60° angle; bore and stroke, 80 × 68 mm; capacity, 4,101.6 cm³; compression ratio, 8; maximum power, 220–230 hp at 6,000 rpm; cylinder block and crankcase of light alloy; cylinder head of light alloy with barrels screwed in; 2 valves per cylinder; overhead, actuated by 1 camshaft through cam followers; 7-bearing crankshaft; distribution chain drive; fuel supply, 3 inverted twin Weber carburetors, 40 DCF type; coil ignition with 2 distributors; dry crankcase lubrication, with tank of 22-liter capacity containing from 10 to 16 liters of oil; water cooling system.

Drive: through rear wheels; dry single disk clutch with elastic hub; gearbox in unit with engine; 5 forward speeds + reverse, II, III, IV, and V, silent, III, IV, and V synchronized; gearbox ratio I, 3.08; II, 1.90; III, 1.38; IV, 1; V, 0.92; pressure lubrication of gearbox with independent pump; axle ratio, 4.

Chassis: steel tubular side frames with elliptic section including transverse tubular beams; front wheels independent suspension, with upper and lower wishbones, lower transverse spring, and Houdaille shock absorber; rear suspension with longitudinal springs and Houdaille shock absorber.

Steering: parallel linkage, screw and helicoidal sector.

Brakes: drum, hydraulic, on 4 wheels; hand brakes on rear wheels.

Electrical equipment: 12-volt; generator.

Dimensions and weights: wheelbase, 2,420 mm; front track, 1,278 mm; rear track, 1,250 mm; tires 5.90 × 16 or 6.40 × 15; weight of car, 900 kg; fuel tank capacity, 135 liters.

Ferraboschi

250 EUROPA

nzo Ferrari has always maintained that an increase in capacity of a sound engine gives good results, but reduction of capacity usually does not. In fact, to produce the 250 type he tried two different methods: starting with the original 166 type and leaving the stroke at 58.8 mm he increased the bore to the limit of 73 mm and obtained excellent results. He did not get such good results by reducing the bore of the 275 type, the head of the Ferrari family of high-powered cars.

The firm's publicity brochure states that the 250 Europa has an engine with bore-stroke dimensions of 68×68. In reality, only a few such engines were turned out: virtually all the touring cars and the small racing sedans of the Mille Miglia type have a classic engine. A subsequent synthesis of these two models did produce the highly successful 250 GT model for touring and racing. The 250 engine was so good that its specifications were later used for the 6-cylinder 1,500 cm^3 racing car.

Since the 250 doubled as both racing and passenger car, it scored high at different levels. The passenger version was popular, increasing the clientele prepared to wait month after month to get a Ferrari. In racing, things continued to go well with the Mille Miglia model. Giovanni Bracco and Paolo Marzotto won a big victory at the 12 Hours of Pescara on August 15, 1952, with an overall average of 128 kph. The next year, the same model won for Nogueire Pinto (Grand Prix of Portugal), Villoresi (Monza, average of more than 175 kph), and Paolo Marzotto (Gold Cup of the Dolomites). The successes of the 250 MM (by now the engine's definitive bore and stroke characteristics of 73×58.8 mm had been worked out) continued until 1954, when the new Grand Tourism regulations favored the high-powered cars. Ferrari had to abandon the 3-liter model to turn toward a heavier type engine for his Grand Tour cars.

Right, one of the many models made by Pininfarina on the 250 Europa chassis. With the 250 GT that followed it, this was one of Ferrari's most successful and long-produced cars.

250 EUROPA

Ferraboschi

TECHNICAL SPECIFICATIONS

Engine: 4-stroke, front; 12 cylinders in V at 60°; bore and stroke, 68 × 68 mm; capacity, 2,963.4 cm³; compression ratio, 8; maximum power, 200 hp at 6,300 rpm; cylinder block and crankcase of light alloy, with cylinder barrels of special cast iron; cylinder head of light alloy, with hemispherical combustion chambers; 7-bearing crankshaft; 2 valves per cylinder, actuated by 1 overhead camshaft per row of 6 cylinders, with cam followers; camshafts and pumps driven by silent chain; feeding through 2 mechanical pumps and 1 self-regulating electrical pump, 3 inverted twin Weber carburetors, 36 DCF type; coil ignition with 2 distributors for each group of 6 cylinders; pressure lubrication; water cooling system.

Drive: through rear wheels; dry single disk clutch, of the Ferrari type; gearbox in unit with engine; 4 silent synchronized forward speeds + reverse; gearbox ratio I, 2.53; II, 1.70; III, 1.25; IV, 1; axle ratio varies according to use.

Chassis: tubular side frames with elliptic section, transverse tubular beams; front wheels independent suspension, with upper and lower wishbones, single transverse spring, and Houdaille shock absorbers; rear suspension with solid axle, struts and longitudinal springs, and Houdaille hydraulic shock absorbers.

Steering: parallel linkage, wheel on left.

Brakes: drum, hydraulic; hand brake on rear wheels; diameter of drums, 330 mm; width of shoes, 60 mm.

Electrical equipment: 12-volt; generator.

Dimensions and weights: wheelbase, 2,800 mm; front track, 1,325 mm; rear track, 1,320 mm; weight of car, 1,150 kg; tires, 7.10 × 15; fuel tank capacity, 140 liters.

375 MM

From 1953 to 1955, sports-car competitions were dominated by big Ferraris with 4,500-cm^3 engines. The rivals called them the "monsters," but could only admire the brutal power of these cars with lovely, aggressive lines. The controversies they aroused were revived in the sixties when the regulations suggested by the organizers of Le Mans resulted in new 5-liter monsters such as the Porsche 917 and Ferrari 512, to say nothing of the 7-liter Fords which appeared at Le Mans and other international competitions for the World Championship from 1965 to 1968.

Let's get back to the Ferraris. With the cars of the 375 series, the course records of most of the classic races were shattered as cars reached speeds on the order of 300 kph (190 miles per hour) for the first time on the straightaway.

The greatest names in automobile racing drove these monsters. Gigi Villoresi drove the 4,500 sports car to victory in the Tour of Sicily in 1952 and the Farina-Hawthorn crew were first in the Francorchamps 24 Hour race in Belgium at an average of more than 152 kph. At Senigallia, it was the turn of Paolo Marzotto, and Maglioli and Hawthorn took the 12 Hour race of

Gonzales and Paolo Marzotto passing the Lagonda 4,500 eliminated after an accident in the 24 Hours of Le Mans, 1954.

375 MM

TECHNICAL SPECIFICATIONS

Engine: 4-stroke, front; 12 cylinders in V at 60° angle; bore and stroke, 84×68 mm; capacity, 4,522.9 cm^3; compression ratio, 9; maximum power, 340 hp at 7,000 rpm; cylinder block and crankcase of light alloy, with cylinder barrels inserted; cylinder head of light alloy, with hemispherical combustion chambers; valves arranged in V and powered by 1 overhead camshaft per row of 6 cylinders, with roller cam followers; camshaft and pump driven by silent chain; 7-bearing crankshaft; fuel supply, 2 mechanical pumps and 1 electrical, with 3 inverted quadruple Weber carburetors, 40 IF/4C type; magneto ignition; pressure lubrication with radiator; water cooling system.

Ferraboschi

Drive: through rear wheels; multiple disk clutch; gearbox in unit with engine; 4 forward speeds + reverse; gearbox ratio I, 2.43; II, 1.72; III, 1.24; IV, 1; axle ratio varies according to use of car.

Chassis: tubular side frames and transverse beams, front wheels independent suspension, with upper and lower wishbones, transverse leaf-spring and stabilizing rod, Houdaille shock absorbers; rear suspension with solid axle, four pushrods, longitudinal leaf springs, and Houdaille shock absorbers.

Steering: articulated parallelogram, wheel on right.

Brakes: drum, with hydraulic and independent circuits; hand brake on rear wheels; diameter of drums, 360 mm; width of shoes, 65 mm.

Dimensions and weights: wheelbase, 2,600 mm; front track, 1,325 mm; rear track, 1,320 mm; weight of car with spider body, 900 kg; front tires, 6.00 × 16; rear tires, 7.00 × 16; fuel tank capacity, 180 liters.

Left, the Ferrari of Gonzalez and Trintignant is serviced as the two drivers exchange information. Above, Gonzalez on the track.

Pescara. In the 1,000-km Nürburgring race Ascari's red Ferrari triumphed at an average of 120 kph. These were the main laurels of 1953.

The following year, while the great powers were seeking to work out a peace agreement in order to restore a little tranquillity to a world that had been badly shaken by far too much conflict, Ferrari continued to win big. His international reputation was such, it was said, that it added to the commercial value of many Italian products, particularly in South American countries. For the Ferrari firm, 1954 was a golden year. The 1,000-km race in Buenos Aires went to the Maglioli-Ferrari duo. Farina won again at Agadir with the 4,900: Scotti won with the 4,500 in Senegal and in Tuscany, while Gonzalez scored a new success at Silverstone with the 4,900. With the same 375 Plus, the Gonzalez-Trintignant team won an epic Le Mans 24 Hour race at an average speed of 169.215 kph. This was a significant victory because it

ended a series of defeats Ferrari had suffered there from the Talbot (1950), Jaguar (1951 and 1953), and Mercedes (1952). Gonzalez-Trintignant beat the Jaguar of Rolt-Hamilton and the Cunningham of Spear-Johnston. The track record in the 24 Hour race was set by Marzotto with an average of 189.139 kph. The Ferrari victory did not end the Jaguar streak; Jaguars won regularly at Le Mans until 1957.

A spectacular success in an endurance race was scored by Umberto Maglioli in the Carrera Panamericana when he drove one lap at an average of 220 kph, perhaps the highest average yet attained in a road race.

Technically, the 375s were directly derived from the engine used in Formula 1 single-seaters. The Formula 1 engine was not used, but three models were developed from it: the 375 America, the 375 MM, and the 375 Plus. Designed by Pininfarina, the car bodies were built at Modena.

Alberto Ascari on the famed Rebuffoni Street grandstand, Brescia, at the start of the Mille Miglia.

In 1954 new technical regulations for Formula 1 went into force: cylinder capacity limit 2,500 cm³ without supercharger and 750 cm³ with supercharger; no fuel limitation (until 1968, when it became mandatory to use commercial fuel); and no weight limit.

After the success of the 500 F2, technicians at the Ferrari firm built a 4-cylinder model which sprang from the F2 engine. From its first test by Taruffi in the Torino Grand Prix of 1952, the new engine appeared destined for big things; but when the tremendously powerful 8-cylinder Mercedes came on the scene the Ferrari plant's counteroffensive was sluggish and the gap was bridged only after a couple of years.

Various types of engines then emerged: the 625, the 555 with increased bore and a reduced stroke compared to the 625, the 6-cylinder 256, and—with Lampredi struggling to find an engine capable of beating the Mercedes—the 252 type with only 2 cylinders which had a high torque.

On the technical racing level, 1956 was perhaps unique: the Ferrari firm "inherited" the racing-car division of the Lancia, including the engine with 8 cylinders in a V at a 90° angle. The finishing touches were put to the Lancia cars at the Ferrari plant and a V8 was mounted on the 555-type single-seater, called Squalo (shark); with the Lancia engine, the single-seater was rechristened Supersqualo.

The technical activity of the Maranello plant gave mixed results, but 1954 was favorable on the whole to Ferrari because the competition hadn't heated up and Mercedes was only beginning its racing activities.

Trintignant won at Buenos Aires, Farina at Syracuse, Parnell at Goodwood, and Gonzalez at Bordeaux, Silverstone, and Bari—none of these victories counting

The Squalo 625 F1 single-seater, modified in 1954. The side gas tanks were important to the lateral stability of the car.

TECHNICAL SPECIFICATIONS

Engine: 4-stroke, front; 4 cylinders in line; bore and stroke, 94 × 90 mm; capacity, 2,498.4 cm^3; compression ratio, 12; maximum power, 240 hp at 7,000 rpm; cylinder block and crankcase in single piece of light alloy, with barrels inserted; cylinder head of light alloy, with hemispherical combustion chambers; 5-bearing crankshaft; 2 valves per cylinder, actuated by twin overhead camshafts, with roller cam followers; camshaft driven by gear train; conical gear transmission for the 2 magnetos on the forward part of the engine; fuel supply, mechanical pump and 2 horizontal twin Weber carburetors, 50 DCOA type; 2-magneto double ignition; dry crankcase lubrication; water cooling system.

Drive: through rear wheels; multiple disk clutch; rear gearbox in unit with self-locking differential; 4 forward speeds + reverse.

Chassis: tubular side frames and transverse beams; front wheels independent suspension, with upper and lower wishbones, transverse leaf spring and stabilizing bar, Houdaille shock absorbers; De Dion axle rear suspension with 4 pushrods, transverse leaf spring, and Houdaille shock absorbers.

Steering: parallelogram, screw and sector, steering column with universal couplings to clear the engine.

Brakes: drum, with hydraulic and independent circuit for front and rear wheels.

Dimensions and weights: wheelbase, 2,160 mm; front track, 1,278 mm; rear track, 1,250 mm; weight of car, 600 kg; front tires, 5.25 × 16; rear tires, 7.00 × 16 on spoke wheels, with rims in light alloy; fuel tank capacity, 180 liters.

Ferraboschj

Above, the Lancia V8 motor mounted experimentally on the Ferrari Formula 1 single-seater for the first time; right, the same single-seater with its original 4-in-line-cylinder motor.

for the World Championship. Trintignant at Rouen and Caen and Gonzales at Silverstone won in title races, but the prize was won by Manuel Fangio, who by now had fully revealed his exceptional skill.

The next year, 1955, Ferrari had few wins, marking the end of the 4-cylinder engine. Once this lean year was over the Ferraris were again in the winner's circle thanks to the technical contribution of Lancia and designer Vittorio Jano and to the great champion Manuel Fangio, who won his fourth world title in 1956. In his memoirs, *My Life at 300* [kilometers] *an Hour,* Fangio recalled that year as one of the most hectic of his career, while indulging in some controversial statements which hardly strengthened the ties between the Italian manufacturer and the Argentinian champion.

Above, the Ferrari F1 Supersqualo of 1956 with an 8-cylinder Lancia engine; left, the 4-cylinder Squalo; right, the Lancia-Ferrari model with lateral exterior gas tanks.

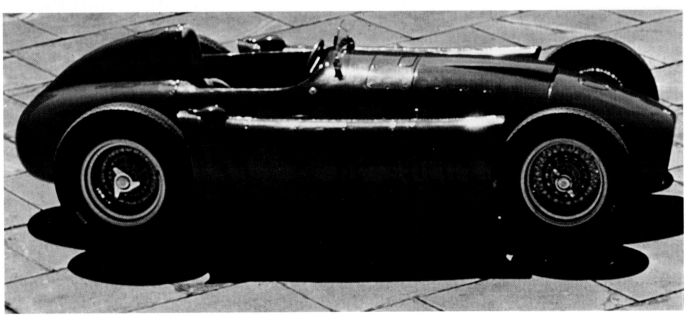

108

Experience gained in formula competition always proves valuable in developing cars for other uses. We have seen it in the past and we find confirmation of it in racing cars with 4-cylinder engines.

These engines were more or less the product of the single-seater F1 and F2. The types with engines equal to that of the single-seater were the 500 (with 2-liter capacity), which used the successful F2 engine, and the 625, which used the Formula 1 engine. The 500 was manufactured in 1954 as the 500 Mondial, then as the Testa Rossa (Redhead) in 1955. The 625 also dates from 1954 and belongs to the Mondial series. In 1956 it was produced with a spider body and was named 625 Le Mans because it was intended for the famous 24-hour French run. As in the past, Ferrari technicians never stopped working on the engines and chassis, so that one new model followed another. With the 500

Mondial there appeared a 750 Monza with similar characteristics except for a bigger cylinder capacity. In 1956 the 8,755, the largest engine with 4 cylinders in line, was built, then the 860 Monza, with a bore and stroke of 102 × 105.

The numbers of the various engines referred to unit capacity until they switched to overall capacity followed by number of cylinders. So far as racing cars were concerned, the new marking system came into use when a 6-cylinder model was built with the dimensions of the 625, at first keeping the 625-type classification. Then, in order to avoid confusion it was rechristened the 376, with the 37 standing for the total capacity (3,700 cm³) divided by 100 and the 6 standing for the number of cylinders.

The 4-cylinder racing car had a particularly brilliant career. In winning the World Manufacturers Championship of 1956, the Ferraris had a long string of victories. Picard won at Marrakech, Maglioli at Imola and—teaming with Hawthorn—in the Grand Prix Supercortemaggiore with the 3-liter 750. Gonzalez won the Portugal Grand Prix, and Maglioli scored a new success at the Senigalia circuit, while the Trintignant-Hawthorn team won the Tourism Trophy. In 1955 and 1956 the most significant victories of the 3,500 were the GP

The car of the Castellotti-Manzon team being serviced at the 1955 Targa Florio. Castellotti, standing at right, is looking at Manzon at the wheel. The drivers finished a creditable third in this race.

TECHNICAL SPECIFICATIONS

Engine: 4-stroke, front; 4 cylinders in line; bore and stroke, 103 × 90 mm; capacity, 2,999.6 cm³; compression ratio, 9.2; maximum power, 250 hp at 6,000 rpm; single-block cylinders and crankcase of light alloy, with barrels of cast iron, screwed into head extending to half stroke; cylinder head of light alloy, with hemispherical combustion chambers; 5-bearing crankshaft; 2 overhead camshafts driven by gears; valve timing, 50° 80° 78° 48°; fuel supply, mechanical pump and 2 horizontal twin Weber carburetors, 58 DCOA/3 type; twin magneto double ignition; dry crankcase lubrication, with radiator; water cooling system.

Drive: through rear wheels; dry disk clutch; rear gearbox in same piece with self-blocking differential; 5 forward speeds + reverse; gearbox ratio I, 2.592; II, 1.929; III, 1.445, IV, 1.099; V, 1; axle ratio varies according to use.

Chassis: tubular side frames and steel transverse beams; front wheels independent suspension, with upper and lower wishbones, coil springs, antiroll bar; rear suspensions with rigid De Dion axle, upper transverse spring and hydraulic shock absorbers.

Steering: parallel linkage, screw and sector.

Brakes: drum, hydraulic; hand brakes on rear wheels; diameter of drum, 350 mm; width of shoes, 48 mm.

Electrical equipment: 12-volt; generator.

Dimensions and weights: wheelbase, 2,250 mm; front track, 1,278 mm; rear track, 1,284 mm; weight of car, 760 kg; front tires, 5.25 × 16; rear tires, 6.00 × 16; fuel tank capacity, 150 liters; oil tank capacity, 16 liters.

Ferraboschi

(Grand Prix) of Senegal (Trintingnant), the Tour of Sicily (Collins), the GP of Rouen (Castelotti), and the Aosta-San Bernardo (Daetwyler). The 500 Testa Rossa won, with Cortese at the wheel, in the GP of the Adriatic and on the circuits of Caserta and Sassari, and with the Hawthorn-Collins team in the GP Supercortemaggiore (the Italian oil firm had discovered sports), and with Phil Hill in the 5 Hour race of Messina.

Many drivers were in Ferraris because the cars from Maranello were the most sought after. There were even gentlemen drivers who paid fortunes to be assured a Ferrari for a race. Another reason for the rotation of drivers was that Ferrari's widespread fame in the country was helped by the presence of a driver from that country on the Maranello team. This is why Ferrari drivers included Argentinians, Englishmen, Frenchmen, Brazilians, Americans, and Germans.

Above, the 500 Sport 2,000-cm³ Ferraris of Carini and Piotti at the start of the first Lombardy Cup race in 1955; right, Eugenio Castellotti at the start of the 1956 Targa Florio.

Fangio driving the 750 Monza.

410 SUPERAMERICA

Above, front detail of the 410 Superamerica; right, the same car, which had a Pininfarina body and the biggest engine produced by Ferrari.

aithful to his principles, Enzo Ferrari decided to use the large 5-liter engine, originally created for racing, on the cars for his distinguished clientele. Naturally, in the passenger version, he couldn't use the power needed for competitions, so performance was lessened somewhat to ensure smooth driving in the lower gears, rather than unusually high speed. The 410 Superamerica, worthy successor to the America type, was turned out by the plant in 1955–56, at a time when in the United States cars with 5-liter engines offered a decidedly inferior performance.

The 410 engine remained in the catalog until 1959, invariably with Pininfarina bodies. It should be pointed out that the versions produced included one called Superfast, the forerunner of a whole series of models known successively as I, II, III, etc. As soon as it appeared the 410 Superamerica was sold to VIPs with season tickets to the Ferrari models, as it were, like the Aga Khan, the Shah of Persia, and Gianni Agnelli.

410 SUPERAMERICA

TECHNICAL SPECIFICATIONS

Engine: 4-stroke, front; 12 cylinders in V at 60°; bore and stroke, 88 × 68 mm; capacity, 4,962.8 cm³; compression ratio, 8.5; maximum power, 340 hp at 6,000 rpm; cylinder block and crankcase of light alloy, with barrels inserted; cylinder heads of light alloy, with hemispherical combustion chambers; 7-bearing crankshaft; connecting rods side by side on thin shell bearings; 2 valves per cylinder, laid out in a V, actuated by 1 camshaft per row of cylinders, with roller cam followers; camshafts and pumps driven by silent chain; fuel supply 2 mechanical pumps and 1 electrical pump; 3 inverted twin Weber carburetors, 40 DCF type; coil ignition with 2 distributors; pressure lubrication; water cooling system.

Ferraboschj

Drive: through rear wheels, triple dry disk clutch, with elastic hub; gearbox in unit with engine; 4 forward speeds + reverse; gearbox ratio I, 2.45; II, 1.72; III, 1.24; IV, 1; different axle ratios as desired by customer.

Chassis: tubular in platform shape, front wheels independent suspension, with upper and lower wishbones, coil springs, and hydraulic shock absorbers; rear suspensions with rigid axle, side guiding struts, semielliptic springs, and hydraulic shock absorbers.

Steering: through independent articulations, adjustable steering wheel, steering on left.

Brakes: drum, hydraulic, through twin Lockheed pumps; hand brakes on rear wheels.

Electrical equipment: 12-volt; generator.

Dimensions and weights: wheelbase, 2,800 mm; front track, 1,455 mm; rear track, 1,450 mm; weight of car, 1,200 kg; tires, 6.50 × 16 on spoke wheels, with rims in light alloy; fuel tank capacity, 100 liters.

![Ferrari logo] 290 MM

The reign of the Ferraris in the World Manufacturers Championship in the years 1952–54 was broken in 1955 by the Mercedes. This spurred the technicians of the Maranello firm to bring out a new car with a 3,500-cm³ engine (the 290 MM), from which came the 3,700-cm³ version (the 315) and the 4-liter version (the 335). In the years they were raced the cars of this series did well, returning the name Ferrari to the top. The first success was scored by Fangio and Castellotti in the 12 Hour race of Sebring. This great victory electrified the Italian fans, who saw a potential champion in the young Eugenio Castellotti. And 1956 was a triumphant year for Castellotti, who scored further successes with Ferraris, in particular in the Mille Miglia averaging 137 kph, under a driving rain that accompanied the triumphal ride of the 290 spider. The car continued to win in 1957. At Buenos Aires Gregory, Castellotti, and Musso spelled each other in the winning Ferrari, and Piero Taruffi won the Mille Miglia, which was marred by the tragic deaths of De Portago and Nelson. This accident, which also took the lives of a number of spectators, led to the indefinite suspension of the classic road race. It was becoming imperative that automobile races be shifted to tracks because the extraordinary speeds no longer permitted their use of ordinary highways. At the end of 1957 Castellotti lost his life while testing a Ferrari at Modena.

Things keep changing and, now that the Ferrari engine had definitely proved better than any other in the racing field, competing firms improved various parts of their

Above, Fangio in the Ferrari 290 MM at the 1956 Mille Miglia;
left, Peter Collins in the powerful Sport 290 at the Buenos Aires
1,000 Kilometer race.

machines. Disk brakes became standard on the English Jaguars and Aston Martins. Important new departures in the field of technology were in the offing, but the Ferrari plant was still inclined toward traditional methods —often with great success as far as brakes were concerned. Ferrari's big bimetallic, strongly finned drums with radial slits, which acted as a centrifugal fan and drew in air in the rear through the backing plate, facilitated cooling. Modified in this manner, the traditional drum brakes were able to guarantee a performance not far behind that of the more modern disk jobs.

Ferraboschi

TECHNICAL SPECIFICATIONS

Engine: 4-stroke, front; 12 cylinders in V at 60° angle; bore and stroke, 73 × 69.5 mm; capacity, 3,490.3 cm³; compression ratio, 9; maximum power, 320 hp at 6,800 rpm; cylinder block and crankcase of light alloy; cylinder heads of light alloy, with hemispherical combustion chambers; 7-bearing crankshaft; connecting rods side by side; 2 valves per cylinder, actuated by 1 camshaft per row of cylinders, with roller cam followers, fuel supply 2 mechanical pumps and 3 inverted twin Weber carburetors, 46 TRA type; twin ignition with spark plugs on each side of head and 4 coil ignitions of 6 spark plugs each; dry crankcase lubrication; water cooling system.

Drive: through rear wheels; aluminum 3-disk clutch; rear gearbox in unit with self-locking differential; 4 forward speeds + reverse; gearbox ratio, I, 2.200; II, 1.565; III, 1.250; IV, 1.

Chassis: tubular flat type; front wheels independent suspension, with upper and lower wishbones, coil springs, transverse antiroll bar, and hydraulic shock absorbers; rear suspensions with De Dion axle, transverse spring, and hydraulic shock absorbers.

Steering: parallel linkage, wheel on right.

Brakes: drum on 4 wheels, with hydraulic and independent circuits; diameter front drum, 360 mm; rear drum, 330 mm; width of front shoes, 65 mm; rear shoes, 60 mm.

Electrical equipment: 12-volt; generator.

Dimensions and weights: wheelbase, 2,350 mm; front track, 1,310 mm; rear track, 1,286 mm; weight of car, 880 kg; front tires, 6.00 × 16; rear tires, 7.00 × 16; fuel tank capacity, 190 liters; oil tank capacity, 20 liters.

■ 246 F1

This 6-cylinder single-seater with 2,500-cm³ capacity was used in 1958–60, right to the end of the formula calling for a 2,500-cm³ capacity limit. Ferraris did poorly on the track, particularly when the Cooper-Climax rear-engine models made their surprising appearance. Jack Brabham won the world championship in 1959 and 1960.

The 246 debuted in Argentina on January 19, 1958. The three Ferraris driven by Musso, Collins, and Hawthorn were beaten by Stirling Moss in a Cooper with a 2,000-cm³ rear engine. Luigi Musso came in second and also at Monte Carlo, once again beaten by a Cooper-Climax, this time driven by Trintignant. The first victory of the new Ferrari came at the Grand Prix of France at Reims, but it was costly, since the French track claimed the life of Luigi Musso. High-speed racing also cost the life of Peter Collins, who crashed into a tree on August 3, 1958, while on the Nürburgring circuit. "It was the only tree in the area where the British driver's Ferrari shot off the track," Richard van Franckenberg recalls in his book.

Collins was a true gentleman at the wheel. One year earlier at the Grand Prix of Italy, when Fangio was the victim of mechanical trouble, Collins willingly offered him his car. Without that highly sportsmanlike gesture, Fangio would have lost the World Drivers Championship, which had been won by the British Mike Hawthorn with a Ferrari in 1958. Hawthorn's success was unusual: he won the world championship without having won a Grand Prix race.

In 1959 the single-seater Ferraris, now equipped with disk brakes, were entrusted to Brooks, Gurney, and Phil Hill. The team was new; none of the "spring team," Musso, Castellotti, Collins, and Hawthorn, were left.

A single-seater Ferrari ready to go in the Two Worlds Cup run at Monza in 1958.

TECHNICAL SPECIFICATIONS

Engine: 4-stroke, front; 6 cylinders in V at 65° angle; bore and stroke, 85 × 71 mm; capacity, 2,417.3 cm^3; compression ratio, 11; maximum power, 270 hp at 8,300 rpm; cylinder block and crankcase of light alloy, with barrels inserted; cylinder head of light alloy, with hemispherical combustion chambers; 4-bearing crankshaft, with cranks staggered to assure the equidistance of the firings with a 65° aperture; 2 valves per cylinder, actuated directly by 2 overhead camshafts per row of cylinders; camshafts driven by chains; fuel supply 3 inverted twin Weber carburetors, 42 DCN type; magneto ignition, with a single machine feeding 2 spark plugs per cylinder; pressure lubrication, with dry crankcase; water cooling system, with pump.

Drive: through rear wheels; clutch, gearbox, and differential in unit at rear; multiple disk clutch; 4-speed gearbox + reverse; double reduction gears and self-locking ZF differential.

Chassis: framework of thin tubes; front wheels independent suspension, with upper and lower wishbones, coil springs, antiroll bar, and telescopic hydraulic shock absorbers; rear suspensions with rigid De Dion axle; transverse spring, and telescopic shock absorbers.

Steering: screw and sector.

Brakes: drum of bimetallic type, hydraulic.

Dimensions and weights: wheelbase, 2,220 mm; front track, 1,240 mm; rear track, 1,240 mm; weight of engine, 130 kg; dry weight of car, 560 kg; front tires, 5.50 × 16; rear tires, 6.50 × 16; fuel tank capacity, 160 liters.

Performance: variable according to ratios used; maximum speed, approximately 270 kph.

Ferraboschi

(Hawthorn had been killed in an ordinary highway accident.)

The new Ferrari team won in France, with Brooks and Hill in the first two places; in West Germany, at the Avus, Brooks, Gurney, and Hill came in one, two, three. But the winner of the World Drivers Championship was Jack Brabham with the rear-engine Cooper-Climax, and he won again in 1960, the final year of the 2,500-cm³ formula. The Ferrari's biggest 1960 win was at the Grand Prix of Italy, with Hill, Ginther, and Mairesse. That year the Ferrari firm did not take part in the Grand Prix of France, Great Britain, or West Germany. It was a period of transition, in view of the new 1,500-cm³ formula, and the technicians at Maranello were hard at work on a rear-engine model. Enzo Ferrari's cel-

ebrated remark, "Horses pull a wagon—they don't push it," no longer had any meaning.

The engines used in 1958–60 stemmed from the 1,500-cm³ model with 6 cylinders in a V called the Dino, in memory of Enzo Ferrari's dead son. In 1958 the 246 (capacity 2,417 cm³) was used and in subsequent seasons its capacity was increased to 2,474 cm³ (256 type). During this period the gas tanks were placed on each side of the cockpit to avoid shifts in the center of gravity during a race.

Above, Phil Hill at the wheel of the 246 F1 at Silverstone in 1959; left, stripped-down view of the 246 F1 showing the chassis and engine setup.

Left, Mike Hawthorn racing hard in a 246 F1 at Monza; above, the long tapered nose of the same car at Buenos Aires.

250 TRS

The name TRS (Testa Rossa Sport) evokes one of the most representative models of the Ferrari racing-car generation. The 250 TRS was the logical consequence of the return to 3-liter capacity for sports competitions. The 250, which sprang from the 166, was first used on passenger cars and then on sports models. It got the name Testa Rossa (red-head) because some cylinder heads with twin camshafts were painted red. The heads with twin camshafts were soon given up, but the name stuck. The 250 TRS began its sports career by winning the 1,000 Kilometers of Buenos Aires in January 1958 with the Collins-Phil Hill team. The two drivers scored again in the 12 Hour race at Sebring, The car's two other important victories were the Targa Florio with Musso-Gendebien and the 24 Hour of Le Mans with Gendebien-Phil Hill.

In 1959, the Testa Rossa had little luck and gave up the World Championshp title, which it had won the year before, to the Aston-Martin. It did have prestige successes, such as the 12 Hour race at Sebring with Phil Hill-Gendebien-Gurney-Daigh. The Testa Rossa got off

to a good start in 1960 with a victory in the 1,000 Kilometers of Buenos Aires with Phil Hill-Allison. After placing well in a number of races, the 250 TRS scored a spectacular win at the 24 Hour race of Le Mans, thanks to the Belgian team of Gendebien-Frère.

The year 1960 closed with a Ferrari victory in the World Manufacturers Championship. Oliver Gendebien, called "the squirrel" because of the way he leaped into his car at the starting line of the 24 Hour race of Le Mans, starred in the winning of the World Championship in 1961. Teaming with Phil Hill, he won the 12 Hour race of Sebring and the 24 Hour of Le Mans, then with von Trips he won the Targa Florio (where the team drove the 6-cylinder 2,417-cm³ model and not the Testa Rossa). The series of Ferrari successes that year ended with victories in the Tourist Trophy (Moss), the 1,000 Kilometers of Paris (Pedro and Ricardo Rodriguez), the 1,000 Kilometers of Spa (Mairesse), and the Tour de France (Mairesse-Berger). The 250 TRS stopped racing after 1961.

The evolution of this car was characteristic of the time.

The original was prized for its elegant, classic lines. In 1959 sports cars were not yet equipped with disk brakes, and ugly ports were left in the front to let in air to cool the brake drums. Then in 1960, after disk brakes were generally adopted, there was a return to classic lines. This didn't last long, since aerodynamic research indicated that cars should be designed with cut-off tails mounting a horizontal stabilizer to increase the rear axle road holding and to minimize the effects of air turbulence.

The classic start of the Buenos Aires 1,000 Kilometer, with a number of Ferraris in the front row.

Ferraboschi

TECHNICAL SPECIFICATIONS

Engine: 4-stroke, front; 12 cylinders in V at 60°; bore and stroke, 73 × 58.8 mm; capacity, 2,953.2 cm³; compression ratio, 9.8; maximum power, 300 hp at 7,200–7,500 rpm; cylinder block and crankcase in same piece of light alloy, including barrels; cylinder heads of light alloy, with hemispherical combustion chambers; 7-bearing crankshaft; connecting rods side by side; 2 valves per cylinder, actuated by 1 overhead camshaft per row of cylinders, with roller cam followers; camshafts driven by chain; valve timing 46° 75° 70° 40°; fuel supply 6 inverted twin Weber carburetors, 40 DCN type; coil ignition with 2 distributors, for 6 cylinders each; pressure lubrication, with radiator; water cooling system.

250 TRS

Drive: through rear wheels; dry multiple disk clutch; gearbox in unit with engine; 4 forward speeds + reverse; self-locking differential.

Chassis: tubular side frames reinforced by a framework to fix and support accessories and body; front wheels independent suspension, with coil springs, upper and lower wishbones, and telescopic shock absorbers; rear suspensions with De Dion axle, coil springs, and telescopic shock absorbers.

Steering: screw and sector, with compensated links.

Brakes: drum, hydraulic; hand brakes on rear wheels.

Electrical equipment: 12-volt; generator driven by timing distribution chain.

Dimensions and weights: wheelbase, 2,350 mm; front track, 1,310 mm; rear track, 1,300 mm; weight of car with spider body, 800 kg; front tires, 5.50 × 16; rear tires, 6.00 × 16; fuel tank capacity, 155–180 liters according to the model.

Performance: variable according to ratios used; maximum speed, approximately 270 kph.

🐎 250 GT

Fresh off the line in 1955, as the logical evolution of the 250 Europa type, the 250 GT had a long life, remaining in production until 1963. For this eight years it was renowned for its competition record and acclaimed as a commercial success. It has played a key role in the history of the Ferrari.

The 250 GT introduced a new type of body, the 2 + 2. The car was built for two persons, with another two "jump" seats in back—less comfortable than the front seats but accommodating two "emergency" passengers. The car was the forerunner of the four-seat coupes which were to sell in great numbers toward the end of the sixties.

All the 250 GT bodies were produced by Pininfarina except for a few cars that were built at Modena by Scag-

Above, the last model of the 250 GT 2 + 2; below left, a fastback in a race; right, cabriolet and coupe versions of the same car.

lietti, using Pininfarina designs. Mechanically the cars were subject to continual technological improvement. As a result the 250 GTs always had avant-garde engines, exceptionally powerful but silent and dependable. The cars were used in races by many drivers, both Ferrari men and independents, until it became necessary to distinguish between the commercial and the racing model. This was when the GTO (discussed later) appeared.

As usual, competition served as testing ground and commercial springboard. As far back as 1955, Edoardo Lualdi, one of the gentlemen drivers who had always driven Ferraris for better or worse, scored his initial successes with the 250 GT. The first big win came in 1956 in the Tour de France, won by the De Portago-Nelson team. Then came an avalanche of wins. In 1957, in the GT (Grand Touring) category, the car was unrivaled and went from victory at the Rally of the Sestrière to the Mille Miglia, from victory at Lime Rock (Ginther) to the Grand Prix of Paris, not to mention the many uphill racers who, thanks to the 250 GT, have scored in the best-known climbing competitions: we can single out Arents, Chimeri, Lualdi again, Giovanardi, Madero, and Lamberts.

The march of the 250 GTs continued in 1958 with such international wins as the 12 Hours of Sebring (Grand Tour category, with the Americans Kessler-O'Shea). The Mille Miglia, now reclassified as a rally instead of a speed event, following De Portago's tragic accident in 1957, was also won by a Ferrari, driven by Taramazzo and Gerini. The classic Tour de France was carried off by the Gendebien-Bianchi team; at Zeltweg, Austria, Seidel won, and Taramazzo won the Inter-Europe Cup at Monza. For the Ferrari 250 GT, it was a big year.

In the 1959 climbing competitions the Piedmontese youth Carlo Mario Abate came to the fore by winning a number of exciting victories with the 250 GT—the Sant'Ambreus Cup at the Trento-Bondone and the Mille Miglia in the Turin Hills. Abate continued to gather laurels the following year, this time in the international arena. He won in his category at the Nürburgring and at Monza. In 1960 Munaron-Todaro won the 1,000 Kilometers of Buenos Aires and Scarlatti-Lualdo won at Targa Florio. These were only the most significant triumphs of the 250 GT, a car bubbling over with personality even in the watered-down stock version which was almost de rigueur for members of the new jet set.

250 GT

TECHNICAL SPECIFICATIONS

Engine: 4-stroke, front; 12 cylinders in V at 60°; bore and stroke 73 × 58.8 mm; capacity, 2,953.2 cm³; compression ratio, 8.5; maximum power, 240 hp at 7,000 rpm; cylinder block and crankcase of silumin, including cylinder barrels; cylinder heads of light alloy, with hemispherical combustion chambers; 7-bearing crankshaft; connecting rods side by side, with thin shell bearings; 2 valves per cylinder, actuated by 1 overhead camshaft per row of cylinders, with roller cam followers, adjustable by screw; camshaft driven by silent chain; valve timing 27° 65° 74° 16°; fuel supply 3 inverted twin Weber carburetors, 36 DCF type; coil ignition, with 2 distributors for 6 cylinders each; pressure lubrication; water cooling system, with pump and fan.

Ferraboschi

Drive: through rear wheels; 2-disk clutch and later dry single disk, with elastic hub; gearbox in unit with engine; 4 silent synchronized forward speeds + reverse; gearbox ratio I, 2.35; II, 1.65; III, 1.13; IV, 1; reverse, 3.05; axle ratio varies according to use and customer preference.

Chassis: side frames and tubular transverse beams with plate reinforcements; front wheels independent suspension, with upper and lower wishbones, coil springs, and hydraulic shock absorbers; rear suspensions with rigid axle, longitudinal springs, lateral struts, and hydraulic shock absorbers.

Steering: parallel arms, independent links, screw and sector.

Brakes: drum, with separate hydraulic circuits; hand brakes on rear wheels (since 1961 servoassisted disk brakes).

Electrical equipment: 12-volt; generator.

Dimensions and weights: wheelbase, 2,600 mm; front track, 1,354 mm; rear track, 1,350 mm; weight, 1,050–1,250 kg according to model; tires, 6.00 × 16; fuel tank capacity, 100 liters.

Performance: varies according to use and customer preference.

400 SUPERAMERICA

The *grands salons* and the *concours d'élégance* of the automobile world took over from the race-track in establishing the 400 Superamerica as king in its field. The car was not designed for competition, but for an ever-increasing high-society market that soon strained Ferrari's production facilities to the limit. Maranello was besieged by celebrities in politics, arts, and sports, checkbooks in hand and eager to get hold of the coveted car with the rearing pony emblem.

The Ferrari phenomenon was very special, and it led to many small shops turning out their own high-price, luxury, prestige cars to meet the demand. But none of them ever had so many famous names among its clients. Ferrari has always been a status symbol; the true celebrities on the Ferrari list have been followed by those who made it on their own, the industrialists, the high-society hangers-on.

The 400 Superamerica model was one of Ferrari's most successful commercial cars—and a beautiful car, thanks to the exquisite lines devised by Pininfarina, who also owned one. The Ferrari firm also built a sports model of the car which served as a link between 3-liter and 4-liter sports types. The engine used was the 330 (the number again indicated unitary capacity) which was previously mounted on the small sedan (the 330 TR) and the

spider (the 330 LE). In this car the Belgian Oliver Gendebien scored his fourth win in the 24 Hours of Le Mans, teaming with Phil Hill, who won his third victory in this race. With this triumph, Gendebien set a record that will not be easy to beat.

The general production model in 1960 came as the logical evolution of the 410 model. The nomenclature indicated the capacity of the engine divided by 10; so 400 meant that the engine of the Superamerica had a 4-liter capacity. The 400 type was the result of fifteen years of development in Ferrari technology; it had the outside dimensions of the first 12-cylinder engine, the 125 type, but with double the specific power (from 50 to 110 horsepower per liter).

A curious thing about this engine was the lack of a maintenance manual. Those who needed the services of a mechanic had to depend on the nearest Ferrari dealer, who made repairs in consultation with the plant. Involuntarily perhaps, the Ferrari firm was following the example of Rolls-Royce with its high-prestige sedan (and its extremely high price) which, it was said, was sold with its engine sealed so that only a mechanic dispatched from the firm could work on it.

This story and others, halfway between truth and fantasy, were just the kind of thing to create an aura of legend around an exclusive product like the Ferrari.

Above, a fastback designed for Le Mans with the mechanical features of the 400 Superamerica; left, a Superamerica cabriolet; below, a 250 GT hardtop.

400 SUPERAMERICA

TECHNICAL SPECIFICATIONS

Engine: 4-stroke, front; 12 cylinders in V at 60° angle; bore and stroke, 77 × 71 mm; capacity, 3,967 cm^3; compression ratio, 8.6; maximum power, 400 hp at 7,000 rpm; cylinder block and crankcase in single piece of light alloy, with cylinder barrels of cast iron; cylinder heads of light alloy, with hemispherical combustion chambers; 7-bearing crankshaft; connecting rods side by side; 2 valves per cylinder, actuated by 1 overhead camshaft per row of cylinders, with roller cam followers; camshafts driven by silent chain; fuel supply 3 Weber carburetors, 46 DCF/3 type; coil ignition with 2 distributors or 6 cylinders each; pressure lubrication; water cooling system, with pump and declutchable Peugeot fan.

Ferraboschi

Drive: through rear wheels; dry multiple disk clutch, with elastic hub; gearbox in unit with engine; 4 synchronized forward speeds + reverse and overdrive; gearbox ratio I, 2.536; II, 1.700; III, 1.256; IV, 1; overdrive, 0.800; axle ratio, 4.25 (at first other ratios were also available).

Chassis: tubular side frames and transverse beams; front wheels independent suspension, with upper and lower wishbones, coil springs, and telescopic shock absorbers; rear suspension with solid axle, springs, reaction struts, and telescopic shock absorbers.

Steering: independent linkages, wheel on left.

Brakes: disk on 4 wheels, with pressure booster, servo-assisted; diameter front disks, 314 mm; rear disks, 298 mm.

Electrical equipment: 12-volt; generator; 65 A/h battery.

Dimensions and weights: wheelbase, 2,600 mm; front track, 1,395 mm; rear track, 1,387 mm; weight of car, 1,280 kg; tires, 205 × 15; fuel tank capacity, 100 liters.

Performance: differs according to variant built.

156 F1

The rear-engine Ferrari Formula 1 cars began with model 156 in 1960. It was produced by the engineer Carlo Chiti, who had come from Alfa Romeo to the Ferrari firm to head its technical center. The first version was a conventional front-engine job in line with Enzo Ferrari's deep-rooted, if outdated, convictions. The new logic won out, however, and shortly afterward a 156 was built with the engine in the rear. The code number once again indicated the capacity and number of cylinders (1,500 cm³ with 6 cylinders).

In its definitive version, the new single-seater had shark-like air-cooling intakes. The car's competition debut was on September 4, 1960, in the Grand Prix of Italy, against the largest single-seaters of the formula then in

Left, the first F2 of 1,500 cm³, still with the engine in front, 1960; above, engineer Chiti next to the first rear-engined Ferrari.

force (2,500 cm³). Driven by von Trips it earned a creditable fifth place. Its engine came from the Dinos and the cylinder angle degree varied from an original 60°, first to 65°, and finally to 120°. Engine power was later increased through the use of direct Bosch fuel injection. Ferrari sought better performance by abandoning the simpler indirect injection.

The clutch was located outside the gearbox to allow better cooling and at the same time to make the clutch easy for mechanics to get at. The 156 was used in races until 1964, when 8-cylinder and 12-cylinder engines took over.

The story of the 6-cylinder models has its high points. Above all it contains the first and, for the moment, only World Drivers Champion from the United States, Phil Hill. Tall, lanky, serious Hill had a special way of psyching up for races. He absorbed himself in classical music. "It helps me concentrate in just the right way," he said.

The day Phil Hill became World Champion was a tragic one for the Ferrari firm. The American wasn't mathe-

TECHNICAL SPECIFICATIONS

Engine: 4-stroke, rear; 6 cylinders in V at 65° angle; bore and stroke, 73 × 58.8 mm; capacity, 1,476.6 cm^3; compression ratio, 9.8; maximum power, 190 hp at 9,400 rpm; cylinder block and crankcase in single piece of light alloy, with inserted cylinder barrels; cylinder heads of light alloy without gaskets, with hemispherical combustion chambers; 4-bearing crankshaft; 6 cranks staggered at 55°, 2 by 2; 2 valves per cylinder, actuated by twin camshafts for each row of cylinders; camshafts driven by chain; fuel supply 3 inverted twin Weber carburetors, 42 DCN type; ignition through 2 spark plugs per cylinder and 2 coils; pressure lubrication, with dry crankcase, radiator, and front oil tank; water cooling system.

Drive: through rear wheels, clutch cantilevered after gearbox, with long drive shaft acting as torsion damper; gearbox and self-locking ZF differential in unit with engine; 5 forward speeds + reverse; gearbox and axle ratios variable, depending on circuits.

Chassis: tubular framework with elements of small diameter; front and rear wheels independent suspension, with upper and lower wishbones, coil springs, transverse antiroll bar, and telescopic shock absorbers.

Steering: rack and pinion.

Brakes: disk on 4 wheels, independent circuits, twin pumps.

Electrical equipment: 12-volt (in some cases 18 volts); directly driven generator.

Dimensions and weights: wheelbase, 2,300 mm; front track, 1,200 mm; rear track, 1,200 mm; weight of car, 460 kg; front tires, 5.25 × 15; rear tires, 6.00 × 15; fuel tank capacity (on sides), 105 liters.

Performance: maximum speed, 240 kph.

Ferraboschi

matically certain he would win the title until he went to Monza for the 1961 Grand Prix of Italy. He had already won the Grand Prix of Belgium and was in excellent position in the world ratings behind the other Ferrari driver, von Trips. In Monza he pushed himself and his car to the limit. Not until the end of the race (though he had passed and repassed the area where the accident happened on the second of the forty-three laps) did he learn that his friend Wolfgang von Trips had been killed, his Ferrari catapulting off the track after a collision with Clark's Lotus. Since fourteen spectators were also killed in the accident, it was indeed an ill-starred Grand Prix of Italy. At the finish line Phil Hill was overcome and broke into tears, even though he had clinched the World Drivers Championship.

All in all, 1961 was a banner year for the 156. Driven by Giancarlo Baghetti it did well internationally. Among other races, Baghetti won the Grand Prix of France, beating Dan Gurney's Porsche in the home stretch.

In 1962 the Ferrari firm put together a squad of drivers consisting of Phil Hill, the Italians Baghetti and Bandini, the Mexican Ricardo Rodriguez, the Belgian Mairesse, and the Englishman Parkes. The Belgian Gendebien was also to race from time to time. But the season was not particularly successful: only Mairesse won a

Above left, Phil Hill and von Trips in the 1961 Belgian Grand Prix; below left, cockpit instruments of the Ferrari 156; right, Innes Ireland in a Ferrari single-seater at Silverstone, 1962.

race, the Grand Prix of Brussels, which did not count for the World Championship. The British cars were showing signs of their coming supremacy.

Meanwhile Maranello had suffered a "brain drain." Engineers Chiti, Bizzarrini, and Galassi, and head accountants Tavoni, Gardini, and Selmi, had left the Ferrari firm. Some of these men were later to put together the ATS, a Formula 1 single-seater. And it was the ATS group that signed up Phil Hill and Giancarlo Baghetti for the 1963 season, taking them away from Ferrari. Ferrari's technical direction was now delegated to the young engineer Mauro Forghieri and the driver Mairesse was teamed with John Surtees, former motorcycle champion and holder of seven world titles. Ferrari's only Formula 1 victory in 1963 was that of "Big John," as the new driver was called by his fans (in Italy, though, they called him "figlio del vento" or "son of the wind"). When Surtees drove his car to victory on the grueling Nürburgring circuit, it was plain he had all the necessary gifts to become World Champion in Formula 1 as well.

Cars bunched on the first turn at Spa-Francorchamps during the Grand Prix of Belgium.

246 P

After the F2 single-seater of 1960, which became the F1 of 1961 (of the 156 type), the 246 P was the second Ferrari to have a rear-mounted engine. The Ferrari people produced two such cars—one for the Gendebien-Phil Hill team and the other for von Trips-Ginther—and they first competed at the Targa Florio in 1961. The other contestants were all in Porsches, the most intriguing of which was a 1,700 driven alternately by four winners of previous Targas—Moss, Barth, Bonnier, and Herman. The duel between the two makes started badly for Ferrari. Phil Hill went off the track, wrecking his Ferrari, and von Trips was obliged to do battle against three Porsches. Oliver Gendebien, who was left without a car as a result of Hill's accident, was sent in to give von Trips a hand. Taking advantage of mechanical trouble suffered by the leading Porsche, the German and the Belgian wound up the 246 P's first race victoriously. Von Trips also beat the track record with 107 kph.

In 1962, the 246 P, which had almost the same specifications as the 246 F1 single-seater, was given a new look involving a series of models with engines of varying capacities. They took their names, as always, from the engine: the first two numbers were the first two numbers of the engine capacity, and the third was the number of cylinders. Thus the 196 type (the predecessor of the Dino); the 248 type (which stemmed from the V8 F1 engine) with an engine with 8 cylinders in a V with a 90° angle and a capacity of 2,458 cm³; the 286 type with a 6-cylinder engine and a capacity of 2,862 cm³; the 268 type with an 8-cylinder engine and a capacity of 2,644 cm³; and the 246 type with a 6-cylinder engine and a capacity of 2,417 cm³.

After rigorous testing, many of these models were discarded, and the Ferrari technicians focused on the 250, 275, 330, and 365 types. These numbers refer to unitary capacity: thus the 250 has a 3,000-cm³ engine (250 × 12 cylinders), the 275 a 3,300-cm³ engine, the 330 a 4,000-cm³ engine, and the 365 a 4,400-cm³ engine.

The racing achievements of the rear-engined Ferraris confirmed that the new mounting position of the engine benefited the entire engine-body-chassis complex. In 1962, the car won the Targa Florio with Ricardo Rodriguez, Mairesse, and Gendebien. This was Gendebien's third win on the difficult Madonie layout. At the Nürburgring in the same year, the 246 P won with Phil Hill and Gendebien, who reached an average of more than 132 kph.

Scarfiotti and Bandini's win in the 24 Hours of Le Mans in 1963 can also be chalked up to this car. They drove a 250 P, of the same family as the 246 P, with a 12-cylinder 310-horsepower engine. The all-Italian success (Ferrari-Scarfiotti-Bandini) was a new departure in the long annals of Le Mans. It remains unique today.

At the 24 Hours of Le Mans race, 1962. A Ferrari sports car leads its rivals, Ford, Porsche, and Jaguar.

153

246 P

Ferraboschj

TECHNICAL SPECIFICATIONS

Engine: 4-stroke, rear; 6 cylinders in V at 65° angle; bore and stroke, 85 × 71 mm; capacity, 2,417.3 cm³; compression ratio, 9.5; maximum power, 275 hp at 7,500 rpm; cylinder block and crankcase single piece of light alloy, with cylinder barrels of cast iron; cylinder head of light alloy, without gasket, with hemispherical combustion chambers; 4-bearing crankshaft; cranks staggered 55°; 2 valves per cylinder, actuated by overhead camshafts; camshafts driven by silent chain; fuel supply 3 inverted twin Weber carburetors, 42 DC type; coil ignition, with 2 distributors and 2 coils; 2 spark plugs per cylinder; pressure lubrication, with radiator and a separate tank for oil; water cooling system without fan.

Drive: through rear wheels; multiple disk clutch; gearbox and differential in unit with engine; self-locking differential; 5 forward speeds + reverse; gearbox and axle ratios vary depending on use of car.

Chassis: tubular framework, with elements of small diameter; front and rear wheels independent suspension, with upper and lower wishbones, coil springs, transverse anti-roll bar, and telescopic shock absorbers.

Steering: rack and pinion, with symmetrical arms.

Brakes: disk on 4 wheels, hydraulic; hand brake on rear wheels; disks perforated radially to facilitate cooling.

Electrical equipment: 12-volt; generator.

Dimensions and weights: wheelbase, 2,320 mm; front track, 1,310 mm; rear track, 1,300 mm; dry weight, 750 kg; front tires, 5.50 × 15; rear tires, 7.00 × 15; fuel tank capacity, 120 liters.

Performance: maximum speed, 270 kph.

Left, the car that won the 1963 24 Hours of Le Mans with its Italian team of Scarfiotti and Bandini; above, Ricardo Rodriguez's car being refueled during the 1962 Targa Florio, which it won; below, the same model with front engine.

Panoramic view of the Monza course during sports-car competition.

158

![Ferrari logo] 250 GTO

A telegram can be responsible for the name of an automobile. The 250 GTO was originally called simply the 250 GT. The "O" came later. All true competition cars have to be officially homologated—that is, approved—from which comes that "O," the first letter in the Italian word *omologazione*. But nothing keeps the makers from selling cars that haven't been homologated. So when the technical committee of the Fédération Internationale de l'Automobile confirmed that the Ferrari in question met the requirements, the firm sent all its customers who had purchased the car and were thinking of using it in races a brief telegram reading: "CAR 250 GTO." This gave the car its name—one now in common use by other firms to give their top lines a certain amount of class.

The 250 had the engine in front and the body was the work of Scaglietti, from a sketch by Pininfarina. Designed from a need to give his clientele a "sports" car worthy of replacing the 250, which had become a "2 + 2," and manufactured from 1962 to 1964, the 250

Left, the 250 GTO fastback that took second place at Le Mans in 1963; above, the 1964 model shows improvements in body and styling.

GTO was the last Ferrari racing car with the engine in front. It was a fitting swan song. For three straight years the 250 GTO won the World Manufacturers Championship, category Grand Tourism. It was a winner from first to last: only new regulations which opened the way to cars with twice its capacity took the 250 off the scene.

The 250 GTO won so many races that we do not have space to list them all. We will point only to the 1962 victories of Abate in the Auvergne Trophy and of von Csazy at the Nürburgring; in 1963 the successes of Rodriguez at Daytona, of Penske and Pabst at Sebring, of Noblet and Guichet in the 6 Hour race of Dakar, of Bulgari and Grana in the Targa Florio, and once again of Abate at Auvergne. Then there was the splendid success of Mike Parkes at the Inter-Europe Cup, with an average of more than 193 kph. The year drew to a close with the victory of Guichet-Behra in the prestigious Tour de France. In 1964 the list of wins was still longer, thanks to Piper-Rodriguez (Sebring), Ferlaine-Taramazzo (Targa Florio), Graham Hill (Tourist Trophy), Parkes-Guichet (1,000 Kilometers of the Nürburgring, Grand Tour category), Parkes-Scarfiotti (12 Hour race of Reims), Vaccarella (Inter-Europe at Monza), Bianchi-Berger (Tour de France), and Rodriguez-Schlesser (1,000 Kilometers of Paris).

The Mike Parkes mentioned above is a British engineer-driver who after a long stay at the Rootes firm came to work for Ferrari early in 1963. While with Rootes he had been part of the study team that designed the Sunbeam Talbot, the Humber Hawk, and the Sunbeam Rapier, all Rootes Group cars. From the competitive standpoint the best assessment of Parkes (and one which opened the doors of Maranello for him) was that of Colonel Hoare, the Ferrari representative in the British Isles: "Mike is one of the best, if not *the* best, of the Grand Touring category drivers. In addition to his outstanding qualities as driver, he has a technical background that enables him to get the best possible performance out of whatever car he is given to drive. One does not often find a driver who knows exactly what changes must be made in a car to make it run better. Best of all, Mike never loses his cool."

At the end of 1962, partly on a basis of this judgment of Colonel Hoare, Parkes flew to Maranello to sign a three-year contract with the Ferrari firm. The automobile industry of Great Britain thus lost an exceptionally valuable talent.

250 GTO

TECHNICAL SPECIFICATIONS

Engine: 4-stroke, front; 12 cylinders in V at 60° angle; bore and stroke, 73 × 58.8 mm; capacity, 2,953.2 cm³; compression ratio, 9.2; maximum power, 270 hp at 7,500 rpm; cylinder block and crankcase in same piece of light alloy, with cylinder barrels of cast iron; cylinder head of light alloy, with hemispherical combustion chambers; 7-bearing crankshaft; connecting rods side by side; 2 valves per cylinder actuated by 1 overhead camshaft per row of cylinders, with roller cam followers: camshafts driven by silent chain; valve timing 46° 75° 70° 40°; fuel supply 6 inverted twin Weber carburetors, 38 DCN type; coil ignition, with 2 distributors for 6 cylinders

Ferraboschj

ach; pressure lubrication, with radiator or oil; water
ooling system, with pump, without fan.

rive: through rear wheels; dry single disk clutch, with
lastic hub; 5 silent synchronized forward speeds +
everse, V direct; axle ratio varies according to use of
ar.

hassis: tubular side frames and crossbeams of various
iameters; front wheels independent suspension, with
pper and lower wishbones, coil springs, transverse anti-
oll bar, and telescopic shock absorbers, rear suspen-
ion with solid axle, coil springs, and telescopic shock
bsorbers.

Steering: articulated parallelogram, worm screw and
sector.

Brakes: disk on 4 wheels, hydraulic; hand brake on rear
wheels.

Electrical equipment: 12-volt; generator.

Dimensions and weights: wheelbase, 2,400 mm; front
track, 1,354 mm; rear track, 1,350 mm; weight, 1,060 kg;
tires, 185 × 15; fuel tank capacity, 130 liters.

Performance: maximum speed, 240 kph.

![Ferrari horse logo] 250 LM

The victory of the 250 P at Le Mans in 1963 was deservedly celebrated at Maranello. The small sedan modeled after the 250 P was christened 250 LM, the two letters standing for Le Mans. Mounting the 12-cylinder engine in the rear of the car required considerable study and testing of chassis and gearbox. Body maker Pininfarina was called in to solve a number of aerodynamic problems connected with noise and cooling. The car appeared in 1964 with the 250-type engine; later on, the 275 engine was mounted on the same chassis. Though it had not yet won official endorsement, the car could adopt the different engine, since capacity had been liberalized. The engine, with unit capacity of 273.8 (which explains the numbering, rounded to 275), corresponded to an overall capacity of 3,285.7 cm³. Nevertheless the model has kept its original name, 250 LM

In 1966 strict regulations demanded that a certain number of cars be built the same year before a particular model could qualify for certification in the racing category. This red tape provoked a violent quarrel and bitter recriminations between Enzo Ferrari and the CSAI (the Commissione Sportiva Automobilistica Italiana), which ended with Ferrari's sending back his builder's license. Then the Italian machines entered a number of races, not in their traditional Ferrari red, but striped in white and blue for Chinetti's NART (North American Racing Team) group.

Before competing in white and blue, however, the 250 LMs gave considerable satisfaction, their most spectacu-

lar victory being least expected. A 250 LM with a 275-type engine, driven by Rindt and Gregory, won the 24 Hour race of Le Mans in 1965 after the big-caliber Ferraris and Fords had disappeared from the scene. "At the beginning of the race those two lunatics are in fifteenth place," Chinetti, the owner of the car, still recalls, "and then they start whipping the 250 unbelievably. Each time they stopped at the pit I saw the rpm indicator on 9,000, while the limit should have been at most 7,500. But believe it or not those two wild men gave me one of the greatest thrills I've had since I won my last 24 Hour race in 1949."

Aside from this win, the 250, though it had not been approved to race with the Grand Touring and therefore

The grandstand at the 24 Hours of Le Mans a few hours before the start of the classic endurance competition.

had to race with the prototypes, won other laurels. In Italy, one of the Ferrari firm's most loyal clients, Edoardo Lualdi, scored with the 250 LM in a series of climbing competitions (Gallenga Cup, Vezzano-Casina, Volterra Cup, Asiago Cup, the Mendola, Predappio-Rocca delle Camminate, Trieste-Opicina, Stallavena-Boscochiesanuova, Cividale-Castelmonte). Mairesse (after his recovery from the bad accident he had at Le Mans in 1963, where his Ferrari caught fire), Bettoja, Toppetti, Nicodemi, Casoni, Taramazzo, Vaccarella, Scarfiotti, and others also won. But now the career of the 250 LM, which in its touring version had had other "interpretations" from Pininfarina, came to an end because the power gap separating it from rival cars had become too wide.

250 LM

TECHNICAL SPECIFICATIONS

Engine: 4-stroke, rear; 12 cylinders in V at 60° angle; bore and stroke, 73 × 58.8 mm; capacity, 2,953.2 cm³; compression ratio, 9.7; maximum power, 300 hp at 7,500 rpm; cylinder block and crankcase in single piece of light alloy, with inserted cylinder barrels; cylinder head of light alloy, with hemispheric combustion chambers; 7-bearing crankshaft; connecting rods side by side; 2 valves per cylinder, actuated by 1 overhead camshaft for each row of cylinders, with roller cam followers; camshafts driven by silent chain; valve timing 46° 75° 70° 40°; fuel supply with twin pumps and 3 inverted twin Weber carburetors, 38 DCN type; coil ignition, with 2 distributors for 6 cyl-

Ferraboschi

inders each; lubrication with radiator and oil tank; water cooling system.

Drive: through rear wheels; single disk or multiple disk clutch; gearbox in unit with engine and self-locking ZF differential; 5 forward speeds + reverse; rapid, silent-shifting Northorn gearbox, lubrication of gearbox through gear pump; gearbox and axle ratios vary according to use.

Chassis: tubular framework with tubes of 35 mm; front and rear wheels independent suspension, with upper and lower wishbones, coil springs, antiroll bars, and tele-scopic shock absorbers.

Steering: rack and pinion.

Brakes: disk on 4 wheels, hydraulic; with separate hydrau-lic circuits, without servobrake; hand brake on rear wheels.

Electrical equipment: 12-volt; alternator.

Dimensions and weights: wheelbase, 2,400 mm; front track, 1,350 mm; rear track, 1,340 mm; weight, 850 kg; front tires, 5.50 × 15; rear tires, 7.00 × 15; fuel tank capacity, 130 liters.

Performance: maximum speed, 290 kph.

330 GT 2 + 2

Meanwhile, in the commercial division a worthy substitute was sought for the 250 GT 2 + 2 model. The 12-cylinder engine was versatile, but had its limits when high power was called for and low-speed torque limited shifting. That is why the Maranello designers dreamed up the 330 GT 2 + 2. The 330-type engine was capable of developing in the neighborhood of 300 horsepower at a lower level of revolutions than the 250 type. The gearbox, which at first had four speeds forward and overdrive, was replaced in 1965 with five-speed manual controls. The body style, once again the work of Pininfarina, changed little from 1964 to 1966. It had single rather than double headlights and a different kind of grille in the side air vents; the spoke rims were replaced with a more modern type in a light alloy.

The 330 GT 2 + 2 type was designed simply to meet the demands of the clientele. As with the preceding Ferrari models, this car was sought after by people prominent in industry and the arts, and by royal families such as Bernard of Holland and Bertil of Sweden. The Ferrari firm won many a cup in *concours d'élégance,* wonderfully glamorous occasions in which stunning models complete a beautiful portrait by gladly posing next to the glitteringly impressive Ferraris. In the same vein, the famous house of Dior always dedicates one of its models to a Ferrari at the yearly showing.

Maranello soon became more and more of a tourist attraction. It was no longer visited merely by those who wanted to buy Ferraris, but also by soccer teams, theatrical companies, and representatives of foreign sports associations. The plant was an "in" sightseeing must. How proud the tourist who can return home and say, "You know, I've been to the factory where they make those great Ferrari cars . . ."

Above, front view of the 330 GT 2 + 2; right, the 330 GO coupe with the same mechanical specifications except for the chassis with a shortened 2400 mm wheelbase.

168

330 GT 2+2

Ferraboschj

TECHNICAL SPECIFICATIONS

Engine: 4-stroke, front; 12 cylinders in V at 60°; bore and stroke, 77 × 71 mm; capacity, 3,967.4 cm³; compression ratio, 8.8; maximum power, 300 hp at 6,600 rpm; cylinder block and crankcase in single piece of light alloy, with cylinder barrels of cast iron; cylinder head of light alloy with hemispherical combustion chambers; 7-bearing crankshaft; connecting rods side by side; 2 valves per cylinder, actuated by 1 overhead camshaft per row of cylinders, with roller cam followers; camshafts driven by silent chain; valve timing 27° 65° 74° 16°; fuel supply 3 inverted twin Weber carburetors, 40 DCZ 6 type; coil ignition, with 2 distributors for 6 cylinders each; pressure lubrication; water cooling system, with pump, fan, and electromagnetic coupling.

Drive: through rear wheels; dry single disk clutch, with elastic hub; gearbox in unit with engine; 5 silent, synchronized forward speeds + reverse; gearbox ratio I, 2.536; II, 1.770; III, 1.256; IV, 1; V, 0.778; normal axle ratio, 4.250.

Chassis: large diameter tubular side frames and tubular crossbeams; front wheels independent suspension, with upper and lower wishbones, coil springs, antiroll bar, and telescopic shock absorbers; rear suspension with solid axle, longitudinal springs, stress rods, and telescopic shock absorbers with coil springs, coaxial with shock absorbers.

Steering: screw and sector, with independent sections.

Brakes: disk on 4 wheels, actuated by twin pumps, with separate circuits and servobrake; hand brakes on rear wheels.

Electrical equipment: 12-volt; alternator.

Dimensions and weights: wheelbase, 2,650 mm; front track, 1,397 mm; rear track, 1,389 mm; weight, 1,380 kg; tires, 205 × 15; fuel tank capacity, 90 liters.

Performance: maximum speed in I, 84 kph; II, 125 kph; III, 169 kph; IV, 212 kph; V, 245 kph.

Just as his *Le mie gioie terribili* became a best seller, Enzo Ferrari found a ray of light at the end of the long Formula 1 tunnel after the trying years of British domination. Living up to his driving talent, John Surtees—Ken Tyrrell had suggested he give up motorcycles for the single-seaters—won two Grand Prix (West Germany and Italy) and the World Drivers Championship at the end of the season.

Surtees owed much to Lorenzo Bandini, his teammate in the 1964 season, who gave him a helping hand on a number of occasions with his adroit teamwork. It was Bandini who neutralized Graham Hill in the final and decisive world drivers race in Mexico.

The 1964 season ended with the Ferraris wearing the white and blue of the North American Racing Team rather than their usual red. The change in color, as we have pointed out, was the result of Enzo Ferrari's pique at Italian racing authorities who, he felt, were guilty of not have properly defended his firm on the international scene. Traditional colors aside, the triumph of John Surtees and the dedication of Bandini were two positive developments coming at the end of a racing year that saw the debut of the new Formula 1 single-seater, the 158.

The new single-seater had a bearing chassis of double wall aluminum plate, instead of the usual tubular frame, and a V8, 90° engine. Projected plans for a Ferrari F1

Left, Lorenzo Bandini as test driver helping to prepare Ferraris for competition. Here he is with the technician Rocchi, back to camera.

with a tubular chassis and a transverse rear engine had been abandoned. The finishing touches were put to the injection system of the V8 engine by the Ferrari's new generation of technicians: Forghieri, Rocchi, Bussi, and May. Two of the single-seaters were allotted to Surtees and Bandini, and a third was prepared with a 12-cylinder engine. Experiments were made with different angles for the V: 90° and 180° (flat, that is). In the end 180° prevailed, but took a long while to perfect.

The 158 first raced on April 12, 1964, on the circuit at Syracuse. And Surtees drove it immediately to success. In the contest for the world title, the Ferraris had their ups and downs, which wasn't surprising, since it is difficult for a new model to reach top performance on the first try. Nevertheless, thanks to some good driving and triumphs in the Grand Prix of West Germany and Italy, Surtees had the highest score, reversing the outcome of the last two competitions (United States and Mexico), and defeating Graham Hill and Jim Clark.

At the end of 1964, Lorenzo Bandini had used the 12-cylinder 1,500. It looked like just the right car to defend his title in 1965, but things did not go as expected. After a promising beginning in the Grand Prix of South Africa (Surtees in second place), things soured and improvements were slow in coming. With the 8-cylinder model now too slow, delay in perfecting the 12-cylinder car plus Surtees being badly injured in the season's final phase (an accident in Canada in a Can-Am car) brought the year to an end on a negative note for the Italian single-seater. In any event, the single-seaters were soon to be taken back to the garage, for with the end of 1965 the 1,500-cm³ Formula 1 disappeared. Beginning in 1966, the racing was to be done in the new 3-liter Formula 1.

158 F1

TECHNICAL SPECIFICATIONS

Engine: 4-stroke, rear; 8 cylinders in V at 90°; bore and stroke, 67 × 52.8 mm; capacity, 1,489.3 cm³; compression ratio, 9.8; maximum power, 210 hp at 11,000 rpm; cylinder block and crankcase in single section of light alloy, with inserted cylinder barrels; cylinder head of light alloy, with hemispherical combustion chambers, without gaskets; 5-bearing crankshaft; connecting rods side by side; 2 valves per cylinder, actuated by twin camshafts for each row of cylinders; camshafts driven by silent chain; fuel supply Bosch-type direct injection, with injectors in cylinder block; coil ignition, with 2 distributors and 4 coils; 2 spark plugs per cylinder; pressure lubrication with dry crankcase; water cooling system, with pump; injection

Ferraboschj

pump drive with toothed belt; alternator mounted on end of camshaft.

Drive: through rear wheels; dry multiple disk clutch; gearbox in unit with engine; 5 forward speeds, with rapid frontal-teeth shifting + reverse (6 or 7 speeds on request); varying ratios according to use; self-locking differential.

Chassis: bearing body of aluminum plate and steel frame; front wheels independent suspension, with upper and lower wishbones, coil springs inside the body, transverse antiroll bar, and telescopic shock absorbers coaxial with the springs; rear suspension with independent wheels, coil springs, transverse arms, reaction struts, and telescopic shock absorbers.

Steering: rack and pinion.

Brakes: disk on 4 wheels, hydraulic, with servobrakes.

Electrical equipment: 12-volt; alternator.

Dimensions and weights: wheelbase, 2,380 mm; front track, 1,369 mm; rear track, 1,350 mm; weight of car, 460 kg; front tires, 5.50 × 13; rear tires, 7.00 × 13; fuel tank capacity, 125 liters.

Performance: maximum speed, 260 kph.

Lorenzo Bandini at the wheel of the Ferrari single-seater in 1966 when Formula 1 was limited to 3 liters.

Above, Lorenzo Bandini in the Formula 1 Ferrari of 1965 with a V8 engine at a 90° angle; right, three views of the Grand Prix of Italy at Monza, with Nino Vaccarella in car no. 6 and John Surtees in car no. 2.

![Ferrari logo] 500 SUPERFAST

When he stopped in front of the Ferrari exhibit, which displayed the 500 Superfast among other models, General de Gaulle once expressed his admiration for the Italian cars, saying: "You people build the most famous sports cars, and this is something everybody would like to do."

It is no accident that the 500 prompted such a statement. Among the many cars turned out at Maranello, the 500 Superfast is a model that evokes the personality and spirit of the most traditional Ferraris in unmistakable fashion.

Put on the market in 1964 to take the place of the 400 Superamerica, the 500 Superfast has a story all its own. In 1959 a single model was built for an American customer and it was called the 410 Superfast. It had a normal Superamerica type chassis, though shortened 20 cm, and was equipped with a 12-cylinder, 5-liter engine. Five years later, the same model was brought out again in a limited series, with decidedly superior performance for a passenger car. The engine stemmed from the Formula 1 engine of 1950–51: the family of engines with a 68-mm stroke. This automobile, which had been created to please a wealthy client, became one of the main attractions in the great international automobile salons of 1964.

Listed in the Ferrari catalog until the end of 1966, it cost over $19,000 and delivery took a year.

A very special and practically unique version mounted on a Superfast chassis. The specifications of this model include a high-performance engine mated to a shortened chassis.

TECHNICAL SPECIFICATIONS

Engine: 4-stroke, front; 12 cylinders in V at 60° angle; bore and stroke, 88 × 68 mm; capacity, 4,962.8 cm³; compression ratio, 8.8; maximum power, 400 hp at 6,500 rpm; cylinder block and crankcase in single piece of light alloy, with cylinder barrels of cast iron; cylinder head of light alloy, with hemispherical combustion chambers; 7-bearing crankshaft; connecting rods side by side; 2 valves per cylinder, actuated by 1 overhead camshaft per row of cylinders, with roller cam followers; camshafts driven by silent chain; fuel supply 3 inverted twin Weber carburetors, 40 DCZ 6 type; coil ignition with 2 distributors for 6 cylinders each; pressure lubrication, with oil in the crankcase; water cooling system, with pump and electromagnetic fan.

Drive: through rear wheels; dry single disk clutch with elastic hub; gearbox in unit with engine; 5 silent, synchronized forward speeds + reverse, V overdrive; gearbox ratios I, 2.536; II, 1.770; III, 1.256; IV, 1; V, 0.778; axle ratio varies according to requests.

Chassis: large-diameter steel tubes for side frames and transverse beams; front wheels independent suspension, with upper and lower wishbones, coil springs, antiroll bar, and telescopic shock absorbers; rear suspension with solid axle, longitudinal springs, struts, and telescopic shock absorbers with coaxial coil springs.

Steering: screw and sector with independent sections.

Brakes: disk on 4 wheels, hydraulic circuit and twin pumps, with separate circuits and servo-brake; hand brake on rear wheels.

Electrical equipment: 12-volt; alternator.

Dimensions and weights: wheelbase, 2,650 mm; front track, 1,405 mm; rear track, 1,397 mm; weight empty, 1,400 kg; tires, 205 × 15; fuel tank capacity, 100 liters.

Performance: maximum speed, 280 kph.

500 SUPERFAST

Ferraboschj

![Ferrari logo] 275 GTS-GTB

F errari decided it would be wise to bring out a model midway between the 330 type and the 250 GTOs and LMs. The result was the 275 GT, available in various versions—spider (GTS), fastback (GTB), and, later, coupe (330 GTC). The coupe had the 330-type engine with 4-liter capacity and the chassis of the 275 GT models, with a short stroke and independent rear wheels. The engine of the GTS and the GTB, on the other hand, had a capacity of 3,300 cm^3 and a bore brought to the limit of 77 mm. Obviously the aim was to unify the work as much as possible, at the same time easing the spare-part problem. Even for highly specialized factories like the Ferrari, the need to simplify procedures and assist the customer was becoming apparent.

The 275-type fastback, intended for both commerce and competition, hit a snag right off. As with the 250 LM, certification problems arose. Until 1965, in order to obtain endorsement as a Grand Touring, an annual output of at least a hundred cars was required. The production of the 275 GT was considered adequate by the FIA inspectors, but they pointed up the discrepancies between the characteristics furnished by the firm and those laid down in the official certification form. This delayed the car's appearance in races. However, in the 24 Hours of Le Mans in 1965, a car of this type placed third in all categories averaging 200 kph. Other triumphs followed in the Tourist Trophy of Nassau,

with Charles Kolb, in the FISA Cup in 1966 with Giovanni Pessina, in the 1,000 Kilometers of Monza in the same year with Zwimper-Illert, and in the 1967 Grand Tour category victory at Le Mans with the small coupe of Pike-Courage. And these were only the outstanding victories.

Left, front view of the 275 GTS spider; below, the 275 GTB fastback of the same type.

275 GTS

Ferraboschi

TECHNICAL SPECIFICATIONS

Engine: 4-stroke, front; 12 cylinders in V at 60° angle; bore and stroke, 77×58.8 mm; capacity, 3,285.7 cm³; compression ratio, 9.2; maximum power, 260 hp at 7,000 rpm; cylinder block and crankcase of light alloy, with inserted cylinder barrels; cylinder head of light alloy, with hemispherical combustion chambers; 7-bearing crankshaft; connecting rods side by side; 2 valves per cylinder, actuated by 1 overhead camshaft per row of cylinders, with roller cam followers; camshafts driven by silent chain; valve timing 34° 72° 66° 28°; fuel supply 3 or 6 inverted twin Weber carburetors, 40 DCZ 6 or 40 DF 1 type; coil ignition with 2 distributors for 6 cylinders each; pressure lubrication with oil in crankcase; water cooling system, with pump and electric fan actu-

ated by thermostat.

Drive: through rear wheels; dry single disk clutch, with elastic hub; rear gearbox in unit with differential; 5 silent forward speeds + reverse; gearbox ratios I, 3.075; II, 2.120; III, 1.572; IV, 1.250; V, 1.040; reverse, 2.670; axle ratio, 3.300.

Chassis: tubular with welded plate reinforcements; front and rear wheels independent suspension, with upper and lower wishbones, coil springs, transverse antiroll bar, and coaxial telescopic shock absorbers.

Steering: worm screw and sector, with spheric greaseless joints.

Brakes: disk on 4 wheels, hydraulic circuit and twin pumps, with separate circuits and servobrake; hand brake on rear wheels.

Electrical equipment: 12-volt; alternator.

Dimensions and weights: wheelbase, 2,400 mm; front track, 1,401 mm; rear track, 1,417 mm; weight, 1,100 kg; tires, 205 × 14; fuel tank capacity, 94 liters.

Performance: maximum speed in I, 84 kph; II, 121 kph; III, 164 kph; IV, 206 kph; V, 242 kph.

330 P2-P3-P4

And now we return to the racing cars, which according to the diehard fans are the only real Ferraris. The competition for the World Manufacturers Championship became even more demanding when Ford participated. Ford came on the scene with endless financial resources, determined to defeat the Ferrari cars in order to obtain, as Henry Ford II was to say, "all those pages of free publicity in the Monday papers" (referring to the write-ups of the Sunday races).

So at Maranello they rolled up their shirt sleeves and Enzo Ferrari recorded his feelings: "The number-two industrial complex of the world is prepared to challenge the monopoly of victories of the little firm in Maranello, to put an end to racetrack monotony. Faced with such strong motivation, perhaps we should throw in the towel," Ferrari went on, "but after spending a lifetime trying to make it plain that the races are open to everybody could we do it now, when everyone is going back to the source and rediscovering that races are a determining element of progress? With our limited means we will remain at our post and with good sportsmanship welcome the advent of ever stiffer competition, convinced as we are that the finest human triumphs spring from rivalry."

Such inspiring words could only electrify the Ferrari technicians. The 330 P type had already appeared in 1964 and it was derived from earlier cars with a rear engine. But it was in 1965 that the 330 P2 appeared with fundamental mechanical and chassis changes and the stress on aerodynamics. In 1966 it was the turn of the P3, the product of highly advanced techniques. For example, the chassis was strengthened with metal and plastic panels, which, compared to earlier systems, made the car much lighter. The big 4-liter engine gained from

The Ferrari P2s entered in the 1965 Targa Florio, which was won by the team of Bandini and Vaccarella.

many technical improvements—twin ignition, twin overhead camshafts, and fuel injection.

In the competition for World Manufacturers Championships, the 330 P and the 275 P—which we shall discuss together, since it is almost impossible to tell them apart—have always played an important role. The successes scored by these models began with the 275 P of Parkes-Maglioli at the 12 Hours of Sebring in 1964. Then Parkes, this time teamed with Vaccarella, won the 1,000 Kilometers of the Nürburgring at the exceptional average of 140 kph. Then came victory at Le Mans, where Vaccarella and Guichet took the 275 P to the finish line at an average of 195.638 kph.

Vaccarella was a modest young man who always gave his best. "I don't want to overdo it," he said. "I like automobile racing too much, and for those who race, there's nothing like the Ferrari. This is why I remain faithful to the cars from Maranello, even though from time to time I feel betrayed or, rather, neglected." But it was not only from the drivers of the Ferrari team that the victories came, and Vaccarella was not alone in thinking that the Ferrari was the best car on the market. The debut of the 330 P was entrusted to Graham Hill, who drove it to success in the Tourist Trophy; the same moustached driver teamed with Bonnier to win the 1,000 Kilometers of Paris, and Scarfiotti captured the Bettoja Trophy.

In 1965 the P2 appeared. In its 275 version, it won the 1,000 Kilometers of Monza with Parkes-Guichet and the Targa Florio with the all-Italian team of Bandini and Vaccarella. A pure-blooded Sicilian, Vaccarella knew the curves of the grueling Madonie circuit by heart. He set a course record of 39 minutes 2 seconds. Vaccarella had to skip the 1963 Targa because he had had his license taken away as the result of a highway accident that brought him before a judge in Pescara.

The success of the P2 continued in 1965 with the 330 version, driven to victory by Surtees-Scarfiotti at the 1,000 Kilometers of the Nürburgring, and with the 365 version in the 12 Hours of Reims, driven by Rodriguez-Guichet. It was in this year that the three P2s competing at Le Mans dropped far behind with brake trouble, but

189

TECHNICAL SPECIFICATIONS

Engine: 4-stroke, rear; 12 cylinders in V at 60°; bore and stroke, 77 × 71 mm; capacity, 3,967.4 cm^3; compression ratio, 9.8; maximum power, 410 hp at 8,200 rpm; cylinder block and crankcase in single piece of light alloy, with cylinder barrels of cast iron; cylinder head of light alloy, with hemispherical combustion chambers; 7-bearing crankshaft; connecting rods side by side; 2 valves per cylinder actuated by 2 camshafts for each row of cylinders; camshafts driven by gear chain; fuel supply 6 inverted twin Weber carburetors, 42 DCN 2 type; coil ignition with twin distributors and 4 coils; 2 spark plugs per cylinder; pressure lubrication, with radiator and tank for oil; water cooling system, with pump and special type of radiator.

Drive: through rear wheels; dry multiple disk clutch; gearbox and differential in unit with rear engine; 5 forward speeds with frontal-teeth rapid shift + reverse; gearbox ratios I, 2.280; II, 1.790; III, 1.405; IV, 1.155; V, 1; self-locking differential; axle ratio varies according to use.

Chassis: tubular framework with elements of 35-mm diameter and plate reinforcements, front and rear wheels independent suspension, with upper and lower wishbones, antiroll bars, coil springs, and coaxial telescopic shock absorbers.

Steering: rack and pinion.

Brakes: disk on 4 wheels, with separate circuits, internally finned disks with double walls, without servobrake.

Electrical equipment: 12-volt; alternator.

Dimensions and weights: wheelbase, 2,400 mm; front track, 1,350 mm; rear track, 1,340 mm; weight of car, 820 kg; front tires, 5.50 × 15; rear tires, 7.00 × 15; fuel tank capacity, 140 liters.

Performance: maximum speed, 320 kph.

the name Ferrari was held aloft by the NART car driven by Rindt-Gregory.

Teamed with Parkes, John Surtees, who had been hurt in a serious accident in Canada in 1965, returned to the limelight by winning the 1,000 Kilometers of Monza in the new P3. Big John had shown his iron will again, though at Maranello they had never quite forgiven him for that accident, which had deprived the Ferrari team of a first-rate driver for months. This was still the time when Enzo Ferrari demanded full-time commitments from his drivers. John Surtees also drove for other firms, and this had not gone down well. It was in 1966 that Surtees and Ferrari were "divorced" just before the 24 Hour race at Le Mans.

During 1966 the P3 won the 1,000 Kilometers of Spa with Scarfiotti-Parkes. The car was close to winning the fiftieth edition of the Targa Florio when on the seventh lap Lorenzo Bandini, who was leading with his Ferrari (teamed with Vaccarella), had an ugly accident, apparently while passing another car improperly. At the Mas-

The P3 and P4 models. Left, the cockpit of the P3; below, Mairesse's car at the pits in Le Mans; right, the sensational finish of the Ferraris at Daytona, 1967.

etti milestone, a sharp curve on a downhill stretch, Bandini's P3 collided with the GTO of Reale-Marsala, who Bandini was to charge later had not moved to one side as he should have. The P3 reared up, its wheels spinning at full speed, and catapulted off the embankment. Bandini dragged himself out from under the car with difficulty, his clothing drenched in gasoline. He returned to the pit greatly upset but unharmed.

All things considered, in 1966 the Ferrari firm was unable to repulse Ford's massive attack. Ford finally won the long-coveted World Manufacturers Championship, which the Ferrari firm had already won eleven times. The 330 P4 prototype was responsible for the famous rout at Daytona. It was in the American 24 Hours of 1967 that the Ferrari firm paid Ford back in kind, repeating the parade of the three Fords at Le Mans in 1966. The two P4s of Bandini-Amon (a New Zealander taken on at the beginning of the year) and of Parkes-Scarfiotti, and the P3 of Rodriguez-Guichet, finished one-two-three. It was a big win for Ferrari, a big loss for Ford. The Ferrari won the World Manufacturers Championship in 1967, although Ford again won the classic 24 Hour French race. The P4 also won the 1,000 Kilometers of Monza with Bandini and Amon and placed second in the 24 Hours of Le Mans with Parkes-Scarfiotti and in the 500 Miles of Brands Hatch with Amon and Stewart, in a rare appearance of the Scottish champion in a prototype car.

In 1967 at Monte Carlo, Lorenzo Bandini died in the flames of his Ferrari Formula 1. The Ferrari firm had lost a superb, dependable driver. His doggedness at Monza in his last 1,000 Kilometer race was to become famous. He was determined to play hare and hounds: "I don't want them to get the lead," he said. "Maybe they'll fall back afterward, but they'll say they're faster than we are. Let me drive first—I know Monza better than Amon. I won't let them get away." "They" were the drivers of the Chaparral. And Bandini kept his promise: after four laps his P4 was in front and it remained there to the end.

The Ferrari P4 with Bandini.

206 DINO

As Enzo Ferrari tells in his book, his son Dino, who died in 1956, was always more partial to small V engines than to big ones. This explains the name Dino given to the V6 engine in his honor. Ferrari built several models with capacities ranging from 1,500 cm³ to 2,500 cm³. This engine was not basically new. In putting it together the plant used the high-class construction techniques that had already served for the V12 and 4-cylinder in-line engines which, as has been noted, had such fine track records.

The Dino developed in unexpected productive ways during its long life. After its glorious Formula 1 triumphs, first with the 2,417-cm³ capacity and then with 1,500 cm³, it was used again for racing cars. It was with a Dino 196 that Lodovico Scarfiotti won the European Mountain Championship in 1962. Then it became a fixture on rear-engine racing cars. 1965 was the high point of the Dino engine. After the debut of the 166 Dino type (1,600-cm³ engine with 6 cylinders), the firm went on to the 206 (2,000 cm³ with 6 cylinders). And it was with the Dino 206 S that Scarfiotti repeated his 1962 triumph, again winning the European Mountain Championship.

The grandson of one of the founders of Fiat, Lodovico Scarfiotti had automobile racing in his blood; he was passionately fond of climbing competitions, in which he excelled. He won nearly all the important competitions in this specialty, from the Ollon-Villars to the Trento-Bondone, from the Ventoux climb to the Freiburg and the Cesana-Sestrière. And while winning with his Dino he set new records for all of them.

The great success of the Dino engine coincided with Fiat's eagerness to produce a high-performance passenger car engine, and led to an agreement to construct the Fiat-Dino. Now Ferrari could participate in the new Formula 2 races open only to 6-cylinder single-seaters, with the stipulation that at least five hundred engines of the type used in this car had to be built. Fiat understood Ferrari's intent and the needs of the small, specialized plant. Fiat turned out the Fiat-Dinos in record time, first as a spider model, then as a coupe.

The 206-type Dino scored wins in the European climbing races and raced in many other competitions. For one year the Dinos were part of the program Enzo Ferrari had defined at the beginning of the 1966 season with "We'll enter a small car and a big one in all the events that interest us." Racing against far more powerful cars, the 206 acquitted itself well at the 12 Hour race of Sebring (second with Guichet-Baghetti), at the 1,000 Kilometers of Spa (sixth overall and first in its class with Attwood-Guichet), and at the 1,000 Kilometers of the Nürburgring (second with Bandini-Scarfiotti).

Still using the name Dino, the 212 E came along and enabled Peter Schetty to win the 1969 European Moun-

Clay Regazzoni, who made his reputation with his daring driving, looking at the engine of his Dino F2.

196

206 DINO

Ferraboschi

TECHNICAL SPECIFICATIONS

Engine: 4-stroke, rear; 6 cylinders in V at 65° angle; bore and stroke, 86 × 57 mm; capacity, 1,986.7 cm^3; compression ratio, 10.8; maximum power output, 218 hp at 9,000 rpm; made in single piece of light alloy with barrels of cast iron; cylinder head of light alloy with hemispherical combustion chambers; 4-bearing crankshaft; staggered connecting rods, in pairs at 55°; 2 valves per cylinder, actuated by 2 overhead camshafts per row of cylinders; camshaft driven by silent chain; fuel supply 3 inverted twin Weber carburetors, 40 DCN 2 type; ignition with 1 distributor; lubrication under pressure with radiator and independent oil tank; water cooling system.

Drive: through rear wheels; multiple disk clutch; gearbox and self-locking differential in unit with engine; 5 forward speeds + reverse; axle ratio varies according to use.

Chassis: thin tubular frames with sheet alloy reinforcements; front and rear wheels independent suspension, with upper and lower wishbones, coil springs, antiroll bars, and coaxial telescopic shock absorbers.

Steering: rack and pinion.

Brakes: disk on 4 wheels; separate hydraulic circuits for the 2 axles, without servobrake; hand brake on rear wheels.

Electrical equipment: 12-volt; alternator.

Dimensions and weights: wheelbase, 2,280 mm; front track, 1,360 mm; rear track, 1,355 mm; weight of car, 580 kg; front tires, 5.50 × 13; rear tires, 7.00 × 13; fuel tank capacity, 110 liters.

Performance: maximum speed, 260 kph.

tain Championship, raising the number of Ferrari victories in this specialty to three. This car had a 2-liter engine with 12 cylinders.

Thanks to the production of five hundred Fiat-Dinos, the Ferrari firm could enter the European Formula 2 race with the Dino 166 model single-seater. The car was new, while the engine was still another version of the V6 so tenaciously backed by Dino Ferrari.

This single-seater was unlucky. It was raced in 1968–70, by talented drivers such as Amon, Bell, Brambilla, de Adamich, Ickx, Redman, Casoni, and Regazzoni. At the end of 1968, Tino Brambilla won a fine victory with it at Baden-Württemberg. This spurred everyone on. Dinos driven by Tino Brambilla and Andrea de Adamich dominated the Temporada Argentina of 1968. They won three races out of four and de Adamich took the title. But this was about it for the F2. After many trials, the F2's racing career concluded with an ill-starred experiment—the "loan" of the car to Tino Brambilla in the 1970 season.

An offshoot of the same car family, the Dino 246 Tasmania, driven by Chris Amon, was more fortunate. During races in Australia and New Zealand the "kiwi" came within a hair's breadth of victory in 1968, after having twice beaten Clark. Amon came through the following year, winning four out of seven races and shutting out Rindt and Courage in the final standing. The same car, turned over to a local driver named Lawrence, continued to win even in 1970. One victory and a series of second places were enough for Lawrence to beat the big Formula 5,000s which were taking part in the Tasmanian Cup for the first time.

From the commercial point of view, the Dino's track record suggested the designing of a Dino GT. It was built in 1966 and shown at the Turin Automobile Salon. It was not brought out under the Ferrari label—the name Dino signaled the birth of a new make—but it was still the product of the Maranello plant. The new car had the engine in the rear and was of the 206 type. The Dino sedan was quite successful and underlined a new style for the Ferrari firm since the accord with Fiat. In 1969 it was equipped with a greater capacity engine, the 2,400 cm³, and the name was accordingly changed to 246 GT. The body, as usual, was designed by Pininfarina.

With the appearance of the Dino, the market for Ferraris broadened considerably. The day of the movie stars, royalty, and opera singers had passed, and the car had greater appeal to the general public with high incomes. Although the car was no longer a plaything of the rich and famous, its delivery still took months. In spite of stepped-up production procedures instituted by Fiat officials, the Maranello firm still could not cope with ever-increasing sales.

Left, single-seaters on line for the start of an F2 competition, the Ferraris in front; above, Amon, winner of the Levin Grand Prix with a Ferrari, in the second trial of the 1968 Tasmanian Championship; below, the Dino F2 of 1969.

Above, the 246 GT with the 1970-71 2,418-cm³ engine; left, the special Dino fastback with body by Pininfarina shown at the Turin Salon in 1965; right, the Dino competition fastback with body by Pininfarina, shown at Turin in 1967.

Something new was needed for Ferrari to climb back to the top in Formula 1 competition, so engineer Mauro Forghieri and his aides designed the 312 B with a 12-cylinder boxer engine. The car came out just before the Grand Prix of Italy in 1969, did a few laps on the Modena circuit, then returned to the factory. The 312 B had an engine with horizontal and opposed cylinders, derived from the single-seater of 1965 and the 2-liter types built for climbing competitions. The most important innovation was the use of only four main bearings. The car had difficult tuning-up problems initially, but they were overcome by vital technical contributions from Fiat, which in 1969 had entered a joint stock-sharing agreement with Ferrari. The big problem was the crankshaft, which kept snapping. After long study, a solution was found by using a special, costly type of steel.

The car made its racing debut in the 1970 Grand Prix of South Africa, driven by Jacky Ickx; the Belgian was the only one to defend the colors of the Italian team in the first race of the season. At the Grand Prix of Belgium, the second single-seater was ready, and it was driven by Giunti, who was to alternate with Regazzoni. The 312 B finally won in the Grand Prix of Austria. It was a triumph with Ickx first and Regazzoni second, and also the beginning of a new season of victories for Ferrari, including Regazzoni first in the GP of Italy,

The Grand Prix of Holland, 1968. Chris Amon is having the tires of his car changed during the event.

312 B

TECHNICAL SPECIFICATIONS

Engine: 4-stroke, rear; 12 horizontal, opposed cylinders; bore and stroke, 78.5 × 51.5 mm; capacity, 2,991 cm³; compression ratio, 11.5; maximum power, 480 hp at 11,500 rpm; cylinder block of 2 pieces of light alloy, with inverted cylinder barrels; cylinder head of light alloy with flat combustion chambers; 4-bearing crankshaft; cranks at 120°, in pairs; 4 valves per cylinder, actuated by 2 overhead camshafts for each row of cylinders; camshafts driven by chain; fuel supply indirect Lucas injection; electronic ignition with capacitative discharge; pressure lubrication and dry crankcase; water cooling system.

Drive: through rear wheels; multiple disk clutch; gearbox and self-locking differential in unit with engine; 5

forward speeds + reverse; gearbox and axle ratios vary according to type of circuit.

Chassis: framework of thin tubes, with riveted plates acting as reinforcements; engine partly bearing; front and rear wheels independent suspension, with pushrods and transverse arms; in the 1971 version the coil springs of the rear suspension were shifted to the internal part of the car and placed horizontally above the gearbox, in order to enhance aerodynamic features; antiroll bars and hydraulic telescopic shock absorbers.

Steering: rack and pinion.

Brakes: disk on 4 wheels; perforated disks; separate adjustable hydraulic circuits for the 2 axles.

Electrical equipment: 12-volt; alternator and battery; safety switch.

Dimensions and weights: wheelbase, 2,385 mm; front track, 1,586 mm; rear track, 1,597 mm; weight of car, 534 kg; front tires, 5/10 × 13; rear tires, 12.5/25 × 15; fuel tank capacity, 200 liters.

Performance: maximum speed, approximately 300 kph.

Ickx first and Regazzoni second in the GP of Canada, and Ickx first and Regazzoni second in the GP of Mexico, which concluded the 1970 Formula 1 season.

Up to the time of the Grand Prix of the United States, Ickx was the most likely candidate for the World Drivers Championship, since he was the only driver in a position to pass the 45 points scored by Rindt, who was killed during the Grand Prix of Italy trials. "I am almost glad I lost the Grand Prix of the United States," the young Belgian champion said afterward, "because I find it much more fitting that the title go to the memory of Jochen Rindt. He never had luck and, when he finally had a clear track to the World Championship, he did not live to see the great day."

Ferrari's determination to fight back became more intense in the 1971 season. Ickx and Regazzoni were two great assets, but at Maranello they also wanted a third champion, and they found one in Mario Andretti, who up to now had only been available for a few World Manufacturers competitions. The season got off to a spectacular start with the 312 B. In South Africa Andretti won the first title test, then scored another success on an American circuit at Ontario, twice slipping by a champion of the class of Stewart on the same curve. And then there was the new 312 B2, an offshoot of the triumphant single-seater. The car was a big step forward, particularly the chassis, whose suspensions were completely redesigned to better adapt the whole machine to the tires, which were becoming more and more important to racing. With Regazzoni at the wheel the 312 B2 made its victorious debut in Great Britain.

The race did not count for the world title, but it meant a great deal to beat Jackie Stewart, beyond question the best driver of his time.

In 1971, along with the 312 B2, construction was completed on a new 3-liter prototype that was to take part in the 1972 World Manufacturers Championship. Said engineer Forghieri at the beginning of the season, "For the 312 P this will be a year of experiments and tests. We want to get the car into the best possible shape and that's all." Unfortunately the first appearance of the 312 P on a track cost the life of Ignazio Giunti, who during the race ran into the Beltoise's Matra which, absurd as it might seem, the French driver was pushing by hand right in the middle of the track.

The next appearances did not produce winning results. In the 6 Hours of Brands Hatch race, after a series of incidents, the car ended in second place with Ickx-Regazzoni. In the 1,000 Kilometers of Monza, Ickx was obliged to quit the race almost at the start because of damage incurred in a multiple accident. In the 1,000 Kilometers of Spa, Regazzoni ended against a guard rail while trying to avoid a slower contestant, and in the 1,000 Kilometers of the Nürburgring the car had to be withdrawn because of mechanical trouble.

However, in tests, the 312 P always turned in exceptional performances, better even than those of the Porsche 917. "It's a great car," said Regazzoni, "and I firmly believe that in 1972 we won't have any difficulty winning the world title. The facts bore us out, and the 312 P in 1972 won all the races in which it was entered."

Above, Chris Amon's 1968 Ferrari in the pit during the Spa race; left, the Ferrari 312 during the trials for the Grand Prix of Italy in 1970.

Left, Amon's 12-cylinder Ferrari of Monte Carlo, 1968; above and right, an interesting piece of research by Pininfarina, the Sigma single-seater on a 312 B chassis, designed for studying safety features during competitions.

Left, taking a turn during F1 competition, Grand Prix of Spain, 1970. The race has just started and the single-seaters are still bunched; above, Jackie Ickx in a Ferrari 312.

Above, the Ferrari 312 in the pit at Vallelunga; right, Mario Andretti driving the Ferrari 312 B1.

312 P

Formula 1 rules were changed again at the beginning of 1966; no more 1,500-cm³ engines, but 3-liter engines or 1,500-cm³ supercharged engines. Ferrari elected the normal intake engine and built the 312 type: a 3-liter model with 12 cylinders in a V. The first car had an engine with two valves per cylinder, intake tubes in the center, and exhaust tubes on the sides. It was called the 312 A. The chassis was monocoque, with a tubular structure to which light alloy panels were applied.

John Surtees drove the new model to success in the Grand Prix of Belgium. In his yearbook, Ferrari ended some pages on Belgian competition as follows: "With this race John Surtees concludes his association with the Ferrari firm. In 57 races he has entered at the wheel of a Ferrari since 1963, he has won 12, with 12 second places, 5 thirds, and 1 fourth. In 1964 he won the World Drivers Championship with the F1 158 single-seater."

The 1966 season also saw the debut of Parkes in Formula 1, and Lodovico Scarfiotti's win in the Grand Prix of Italy at Monza. "They have gone so far as to write that I won thanks to Parkes," Scarfiotti said in an interview. "It's true Mike helped me by running interference when I tried to get away, but it's also true that I really had to sweat for that win."

At Monza, Scarfiotti used the 312 B-type engine with three valves, which was used again in the 1967 season, though mounted on a new chassis. In the closing part of the season (as in 1966) the 312 C was given a new engine with four valves per cylinder and with exhaust tubes in the center of the V.

New Zealander Chris Amon of the McLaren firm was hired in 1967 to replace John Surtees. He was to race the Ferrari 312 C for the first time at Brands Hatch, in the Race of Champions, but an automobile accident on the way to the track kept him from taking part. The initial success of the new single-seater came on April 29 at Silverstone. It was Mike Parkes who won, on the track where he had begun his racing career.

For Ferrari 1967 was a tragic year. Running in second place in his 312 C at Monte Carlo, Bandini was involved in a terrible accident on the chicane near the harbor. His car burst into flames, and he was killed. Parkes also had a bad accident that year, which kept him out of competition for a long time. Only one Ferrari, driven by Amon, was in contention, and it did not place well.

The Ferrari team began the following season with the 312 C, then with a new version fitted out with aileron stabilizers. This technical innovation, developed by Ferrari, was quickly adopted by his rivals. Meanwhile, the driving team had again been strengthened: alongside Amon was the youthful Jacky Ickx and ex-Alfa racer

Andrea de Adamich. In the 1968 season the F1 had one big win: the Belgian Ickx triumphed at Rouen, breaking a long dry spell for Ferrari.

In 1969 the Formula 1 single-seater engine was again a four-valve model, but with side exhausts and an intake in the center of the V to provide one type of engine for the F1 and its prototype the 312 P. Ferrari had decided to reenter the World Manufacturers Championship, though only on a limited basis. The records of the F1 and the prototype in world-championship events were similar, with 1969 an unlucky year. Deprived of Ickx, who was driving for the Brabham firm, and Adamich, who had gone back to Alfa Romeo, Ferrari could no longer send in a "shock wave" of several cars, but had to depend on the talent of individual drivers.

The Ferrari firm often participated in World Drivers Championship races with only one car; even in endurance races a single 312 P was sometimes entered. Pickings were necessarily slim. The team counted on Amon, Bell (occasionally), Andretti (for a few prototype competitions), Rodriguez, Schetty, and Piper. 1969 was disappointing to Ferrari boosters in Formula 1 events and with the prototype 312 P, of which two models ran at Monza and Le Mans.

Soon people began to say that Amon just wasn't a winning driver. Enzo Ferrari put it this way: "There is no such thing as a lucky or unlucky driver," as if to imply that he had his own opinion of Amon, a true champion when he had the lead, but lacking that rage to win so vital to racing competition. So it was that at the end of 1969, after many letters, telegrams, and telephone calls, Chris Amon dropped by Maranello to say good-bye to his friends before returning to England and a new job with the March Company.

Above, the Ferrari 312 P of the Rodriguez-Schetty team at Monza's 1,000 Kilometer race, 1969; below, the Ferrari of the Rodriguez-Amon team during the Nürburgring 1,000 Kilometers, 1969.

312 P

TECHNICAL SPECIFICATIONS

Engine: 4-stroke, rear; 12 horizontal, opposed cylinders; bore and stroke, 78.5 × 51.5 mm; capacity, 2,991 cm^3; compression ratio, 11.5; maximum power, 450 hp at 10,800 rpm; cylinder block of light alloy, with cylinder barrels inserted; cylinder heads of light alloy, with flat combustion chambers; 4-bearing crankshaft; cranks at 120°, in couples; 4 valves per cylinder, actuated by 2 overhead camshafts for each row of cylinders; camshafts driven by chains; fuel supply indirect Lucas injection; capacitative discharge electronic ignition; dry crankcase pressure lubrication; water cooling system.

Drive: through rear wheels; multiple disk clutch; gearbox and differential in unit with engine; self-locking differential; 5 forward speeds + reverse; gearbox and axle ratios vary according to type of circuit.

Chassis: light alloy sheet metal sections riveted and reinforced by tubular and cast elements in attachment points of engine and suspensions, front and rear wheels independent suspension, with pushrods and transverse arms, coil springs, and telescopic hydraulic shock absorbers.

Steering: rack and pinion.

Brakes: disk on 4 wheels, perforated disks, split hydraulic circuits.

Electrical equipment: 12-volt; alternator and battery; safety switch.

Dimensions and weights: wheelbase, 2,220 mm; front track, 1,425 mm; rear track, 1,400 mm; length 3,500 mm; width, 1,880 mm; weight of car with water and oil, 585 kg; front tires, 5/22 × 13; rear tires, 13/26 × 15; fuel tank capacity, 120 liters.

Performance: maximum speed, approximately 320–330 kph.

512 S

It is an absurdity demanded by anachronistic international regulations," said Enzo Ferrari of the 512 S that the Maranello firm had built for the World Manufacturers Championship of 1970. The twenty-five sport models turned out were the result of a curious decision on the part of the CSI which, in an effort to reduce the dangers of racing to a minimum, imposed a minimum output of twenty-five for the 5,000-cm³ models. This led to starting fields of 500-horsepower-plus "monsters." The Ferrari firm was obliged to build the 512 S to cope with the Porsche 917s of 4,500 cm³ (and then 5,000 cm³) capacity. Then, having gained solid backing from Fiat, the Ferrari racing team from Maranello could continue undistracted.

The 512 S appeared in November 1969. It had a V12 engine with the cylinders set at a 60° angle, and a capacity of 4,993 cm³ generating 560–580 horsepower. Ferrari officially used three cars, assigning them to Ickx (who had returned to the Maranello team), Andretti, Merzario, Giunti, Vaccarella, and Schetty. The 512 S won the 12 Hours of Sebring, with Giunti-Vaccarella-Andretti. Andretti, who had been in the lead teamed with Merzario for a good part of the competition, had to abandon his car just as the race was coming to an end. He was given the car that Giunti and Vaccarella had been driving for eleven hours, and brought it in for the win.

This was the 512 S's only win in the World Manufacturers Championship. Temporary hiring of Surtees and Amon, and the addition of Regazzoni to the racing crew, did not help. But at the end of the season the renovated 512, rechristened SM, scored a victory in the 9 Hours of Kyalami, South Africa, with Ickx and Giunti driving.

Body maker Pininfarina, as with the other Ferrari sports models, gave the 512 S's body an artistic design. The Modulo also stirred up interest. It was a car "idea" with a highly original line, used for the mechanical groups of the 512 S, or the Grand Tourism version of the big sports car. The two cars were shown at the great automobile salons, making a splash for the Ferrari firm.

Since the 512 S was a sports car turned out in a run of twenty-five, according to regulations, there were enough in stock, not counting those retained by Ferrari, to satisfy the demands of interested customers. Moretti and Manfredini were the first buyers, then the Swiss Filipinetti team. In 1971, the American Sunoco team completely rebuilt a 512 S, and Roger Penske turned it over to the Donahue-Parsons team. But by 1971 Ferrari had given up the 512 S to work on the 312 PB, a fleet prototype which, after an absence of four years, was to bring the world title back to Maranello. Nevertheless, as a help to their customers they worked out the 512 M which increased the horsepower to 610 at 9,000 rpm, weighed slightly less, and had several modifications in the chassis.

Above right, the Ferrari 512 S during the 24 Hours of Le Mans, 1970; below, the engine of the car; 12 cylinders in a V at a 60° angle, capacity of 4,993 cm³ with 600 horsepower.

TECHNICAL SPECIFICATIONS

Engine: 4-stroke, rear; 12 cylinders in V at 60° angle; bore and stroke, 87 × 70 mm; capacity, 4,994 cm³; compression ratio, II; maximum power, 550 hp at 8,000 rpm; cylinder block of light alloy, with inserted cylinder barrels; cylinder heads of light alloy, with flat combustion chambers; 7-bearing crankcase; cranks at 120°; 4 valves per cylinder, actuated by 2 camshafts for each row of cylinders; camshafts driven by chains; fuel supply indirect Lucas injection; capacitative discharge electronic ignition; dry crankcase pressure lubrication; water cooling system.

Drive: through rear wheels; multiple disk clutch; gearbox and differential in unit with rear engine; self-locking differential; 5 forward speeds + reverse; gearbox and axle ratios vary according to circuits.

Chassis: mixed assembly of tubular framework and light sheet metal; independent front and rear suspensions, with rods and struts; coil springs and hydraulic telescopic shock absorbers.

Steering: rack and pinion.

Brakes: disk on 4 wheels; perforated disks; separate hydraulic circuits.

Electrical equipment: 12-volt; alternator and battery; safety switch; regulation illumination system.

Dimensions and weights: wheelbase, 2,400 mm; front track, 1,518 mm; rear track, 1,511 mm; length, 4,180 mm; width, 2,015 mm; weight of car, 820 kg; front tires, 4.25/11.50 × 11; rear tires, 6.00/14.50 × 15; fuel tank capacity, 120 liters.

Performance: maximum speed, approximately 340–350 kph.

512 S

The 512 special fastback designed by Pininfarina on a 512 S chassis made with high-tension steel tubing and riveted light aluminum panels.

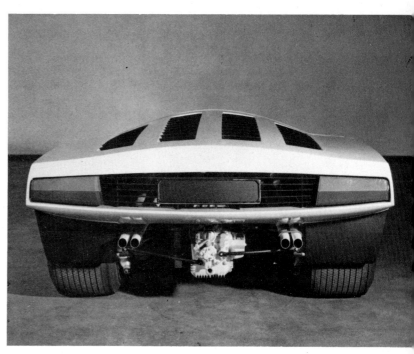

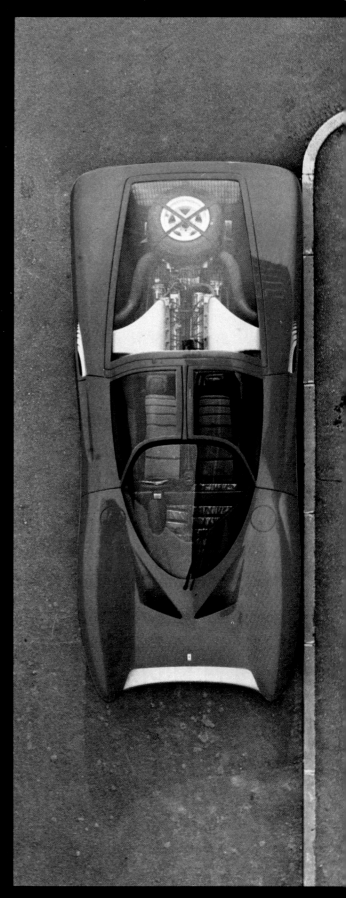

Above and below, the Pininfarina Modulo, straight out of science fiction with interchangeable body elements on a 512 S chassis; three pictures at right, the 1968 fastback prototype 250 PS.

Above left, this model with a B12 engine of 6,222 cm³ and 620 horsepower was prepared for the 1968 Can-Am; below left, Amon driving his Ferrari; above, Andretti in his car which came in fourth at Watkins Glen in 1971.

The 365 GTC 4 coupe, with a body by Pininfarina, is the most recent product of a factory that has undergone sweeping changes since Fiat officials joined the Maranello work force to set up mass production techniques. Like the Dino, the big new car is part of the mass production program. The factory was completely rebuilt and its area doubled to provide space for the manufacture of the Fiat-Dino engine and the final assembly of the 365 GTC 4 in its two versions, spider and coupe.

The engine, with four overhead camshafts, of the 365 GTC (unit capacity again being used in nomenclature) is the last of a series of large racing engines, and the suspension, brakes, and other details come from racing cars, but the body is the result of unremitting stylistic research at the Pininfarina plant, which has created a distinctive style with a pleasing aggressive line that stresses the main Ferrari mechanical features. In twenty-five years of collaboration, Pininfarina has always faultlessly complemented the Ferrari product, never failing to come up with the right body for a given car.

In keeping with present commercial demands for high performance and maximum comfort, the 365 GTC has retractable headlights for a more elegant look, an interior with flawless finishings, a great number of accessories, and all the service controls imaginable—power brakes, power steering, air conditioning, and a stereo cassette, radio, and record player.

Before the 365 GTC the Ferrari plant had begun producing the GTB 4: although this car had no official name yet, people were calling it the Daytona to commemorate the spectacular success of the Ferraris at the Florida race. It seemed a natural, since the famous 250 LM was directly identified with the big win at Le Mans, but this time Enzo Ferrari did not agree to link a car's name to a sporting event.

The range of recent models that led to the 365 GTC 4 coupe; above left, the spider; below left, the 365 GTC 4 fastback, better known as the Daytona; above, a detail of the retractable headlights.

The complex instrument panel and two views of the 365 GTC 4 shown at the Geneva Salon in 1971. Pininfarina's original body-work styling catches the eye.

365 GTC 4

E. Ferraboschi 71

TECHNICAL SPECIFICATIONS

Engine: 4-stroke, front; 12 cylinders in V at 60° angle; bore and stroke, 81 × 71 mm; capacity, 4,390 cm³; compression ratio, 8.8; maximum power, 340 hp at 6,800 rpm; cylinder block and crankcase of light alloy, with cylinder liners inserted; cylinder head of light alloy, with hemispherical combustion chambers; 7-bearing crankshaft; cranks arranged in pairs at 120°; 2 valves per cylinder, actuated by 2 camshafts per row of cylinders, close together overhead; fuel supply 6 twin horizontal Weber carburetors, 40 DCOE type; intake pipes at center of heads, between the 2 camshafts; coil ignition with 1 Marelli distributor; pressure lubrication; water cooling system.

Drive: through rear wheels; dry single disk clutch; gearbox with 5 forward speeds + reverse, in unit with engine; limited-slip differential attached to chassis on rubber plugs; gearbox ratios, I, 2.496; II, 1.67; III, 1.245; IV, 1; V, 0.802; axle ratio, 4.091.

Chassis: tubular with reinforcing sheet metal welded to body; front and rear wheels independent suspension, with upper and lower wishbones, coil springs, and hydraulic telescopic shock absorbers.

Steering: servo-assisted ball circulation.

Brakes: disk on 4 wheels; perforated disks; 2 independent hydraulic circuits and servobrake; hand brake on rear wheels.

Electrical equipment: 12-volt; alternator; iodine headlights.

Dimensions and weights: wheelbase, 2,500 mm; front track, 1,470 mm; rear track, 1,470 mm; length, 4,570 mm; width, 1,780 mm; height, 1,270 mm; weight of car, 1,450 kg; tires, 215/70 VR × 15; fuel tank capacity, 100 liters.

Performance: maximum speed, 260 kph.

Peterson and Redman, both in Ferraris, in the 1,000 Kilometers of Buenos Aires. They placed first and second, respectively.

The new Pininfarina Ferrari Dino 246 GTS, convertible coupe version. Strengthening of the body and incorporation of a roll-over bar have allowed a removable rigid top which can be stored in a special compartment in back of the driver's seat.

SUMMARY OF FERRARI PRODUCTION

The Ferrari single-seater Formula 1, model 312 B2, 1972, with Regazzoni driving in the Argentine Grand Prix.

number	year	model	number of cylinders	bore and stroke (mm)	stroke/bore	ind. cylinder displacement (cm³)	total displacement (cm³)	compression ratio	maximum power (hp)	rpm (engine)	number and type of carburetors
1	46	125 GT	12 V	55 x 52,5	0,95	124,7	1496,7	8	72	5400	3 - 30 DCF
2	47	125 S	12 V	55 x 52,5	0,95	124,7	1496,7	9	118	7000	3 - 30 DCF
3	47	159 S	12 V	59 x 58	0,98	158,6	1902,8	8,5	125	7000	3 - 30 DCF
4	48	166 S	12 V	60 x 58,8	0,98	166,2	1995	8,5	150	7000	3 - 30 DCF
5	48	166 MM	12 V	60 x 58,8	0,98	166,2	1995	8,5	140	6600	3 - 32 DCF
6	48	166 Inter	12 V	60 x 58,8	0,98	166,2	1995	8	115	6000	1 - 32 DCF
7	48	125 F 1	12 V	55 x 52,5	0,95	124,7	1496,7	6,5	230	7000	1 - 50 WCF
8	48	166 F 2	12 V	55 x 52,5	0,95	124,7	1496,7	10	160	7000	3 - 32 DCF
9	49	125 F 1	12 V	60 x 58,8	0,98	166,2	1995	7	260	7000	1 - Weber triplo
10	49	125 F 1 - DD	12 V	55 x 52,5	0,95	124,7	1496,7	7	280	7500	1 - Weber 50 WCF
11	49	166 F L Short chassis	12 V	60 x 58,8	0,98	166,2	1995	6,5	310	7000	1 - 40 DO3C
12	49	166 F 2 Long chassis	12 V	60 x 58,8	0,98	166,2	1995	6,5	310	7000	1 - 40 DO3C
13	49	166 S	12 V	60 x 58,8	0,98	166,2	1995	8	90	5600	1 - 32 DCF
14	49	166 MM	12 V	60 x 58,8	0,98	166,2	1995	8,5	140	6600	3 - 32 DCF
15	50	195 S (MM)	12 V	65 x 58,8	0,90	195,1	2341	8,5	160	7000	3 - 32 DCF
16	50	275 S	12 V	72 x 68	0,94	276,8	3322,3	8	220	7200	3 - 40 DCF
17	50	275 F 1	12 V	72 x 68	0,94	276,8	3322,3	10	300	7300	3 - 38 DCF
18	50	340 F 1	12 V	80 x 68	0,85	341,8	4101,6	12	335	7000	3 - 42 DCF
19	50	375 F 1	12 V	80 x 74,5	0,93	374,5	4493,7	11	350	7000	3 - 42 DCF
20	50	166 Inter	12 V	60 x 58,8	0,98	166,2	1995	7,5	105	6000	1 - 32 DCF
21	50	166 MM	12 V	60 x 58,8	0,98	166,2	1995	9,5	145	7000	3 - 36 DCF
22	51	375 F 1	12 V	80 x 74,5	0,93	374,5	4493,7	12	384	7500	3 - 46 DCF3
23	51	166 F 2	12 V	63,5 x 52,5	0,83	166,2	1995,2	11	160	7200	3 - 32 DCF
24	51	500 F 2	4 L	90 x 78	0,87	496,2	1984,9	12	170	7000	2 - 50 DCO
25	51	212 F 1	12 V	68 x 58,8	0,86	213,5	2562,6	12	200	7500	3 - 32 DCF
26	51	195 Inter	12 V	65 x 58,8	0,90	195,1	2341	7,5	135	6000	1 - 36 DCF

Ignition: S = simple; D = double: B = reel; M = magneto. **Engine position:** A = Front; P = rear. **Gearbox position:** A = front; P = rear; V = overdrive. **Suspension:** B = springs; BT = transverse springs; M = coil springs; DD = De Dion bridge; O = swinging semiaxle; I = independent or transverse parallelogram; N = normal rigid bridge.

Summed up in the following tables, year by year, are the technical data for all Ferrari automobiles, whether made for private customers or for racing competitions. Some of the models, which were produced over a span of several years, appear more than once in the tables, since they underwent modifications. Data whose exactness was impossible to verify (this was rarely the case) are not included. The letters that often follow the model number have the following meanings: F1, Formula 1 (1946–51, 1,500 cm³ with supercharger, 4,500 without; 1954–60, 2,500 cm³ without supercharger; 1961–65, 1,500 cm³ without supercharger; 1966–, 3,000 cm³); FL, free formula (without; capacity limitation); GT, touring; GTB, touring, small sedan; GTC, touring coupe; GTO, certified touring; GTS, touring spider; LM, Le Mans; MI, Monza-Indianapolis; MM, Mille Miglia; P, engine in rear, or prototype; S, sport; SA, Superamerica; SF, Superfast; TR, Testa Rossa (redhead); TRC, Testa Rossa racing; TRS, Testa Rossa sport.

ignition	number of camshafts	engine position	gearbox position and number of speeds	wheelbase (mm)	front track (mm)	rear track (mm)	front suspensions	rear suspensions	front tires	rear tires	weight (kg)	capacity fuel tank (l)	maximum speed (kph)
2 B	I	A	A 5	2420	1240	1240	I-BT	N-B	5,50 x 15	5,50 x 15	750	72	155
2 B	I	A	A 5	2420	1255	1200	I-BT	N-B	5,50 x 15	5,50 x 15	750	75	170
2 B	I	A	A 5	2420	1255	1200	I-BT	N-B	5,50 x 15	5,50 x 15	750	75	180
2 B	I	A	A 5	2420	1255	1200	I-BT	N-B	5,50 x 15	5,50 x 15	800	70	190
2 B	I	A	A 5	2200	1255	1200	I-BT	N-B	5,50 x 15	6,00 x 15	800	70	185
2 B	I	A	A 5	2420	1255	1200	I-BT	N-B	5,50 x 15	5,50 x 15	1000	70	150
2 M	I	A	A 5	2160	1270	1250	I-BT	O-BT	5,50 x 15	6,50 x 16	700	120	240
2 M	I	A	A 5	2420	1255	1200	I-BT	N-B	5,50 x 15	6,00 x 15	700	120	200
2 M	2	A	A 5	2320	1250	1200	I-BT	O-BT	5,50 x 16	6,50 x 16	600	140	
2 M	2	A	P 5	2320	1250	1200	I-BT	DD-BT	5,50 x 16	6,50 x 16	600	140	
2 M	I	A	A 5	2160	1270	1250	I-BT	O-BT	5,50 x 16	7,00 x 16	740	160	270
2 M	I	A	A 5	2380	1270	1250	I-BT	O-BT	5,50 x 16	7,00 x 16	760	160	
2 B	I	A	A 5	2620	1250	1200	I-BT	N-B	5.50 x 15	5,50 x 15	850	75	150
2 B	I	A	A 5	2200	1255	1200	I-BT	N-B	5,50 x 15	6,00 x 15	800	75	
2 B	I	A	A 5	2200	1255	1200	I-BT	N-B	5,50 x 15	6,00 x 15	800	120	
2 B	I	A	A 4	2250	1270	1250	I-BT	N-B	5,50 x 16	5,50 x 16			
2 M	I	A	A 5	2160	1278	1250	I-BT	O-BT	5,50 x 16	7,00 x 16	820	160	260
2 M	I	A	P 4	2160	1278	1250	I-BT	DD-BT	5,50 x 16	7,00 x 16	850	180	280
2 M	I	A	P 4	2320	1270	1250	I-BT	DD-BT	5,50 x 16	7,00 x 17	710	195	300
2 B	I	A	A 5	2500	1270	1250	I-BT	N-B	5,90 x 15	5,90 x 15	900	80	180
2 B	I	A	A 5	2250	1270	1250	I-BT	N-B	5,50 x 16	5,50 x 16	680	145	210
D 4 M	I	A	P 4	2320	1270	1250	I-BT	DD-BT	5,50 x 16	7,00 x 17	720	195	300
2 M	2	A	A 5	2280	1225	1200	I-BT	O-BT	5,25 x 16	6,50 x 16	600	150	230
2 M	2	A	P 4	2160	1270	1250	I-BT	DD-BT	5,25 x 16	5,50 x 16	560	150	240
2 M	I	A	A 5	2280	1225	1200	I-BT	O-BT	5,25 x 16	5,50 x 16	600	150	250
2 B	I	A	A 5	2500	1278	1250	I-BT	N-B	5,90 x 15	5,90 x 15	950	80	180

number	year	model	number of cylinders	bore and stroke (mm)	stroke/bore	ind. cylinder displacement (cm³)	total displacement (cm³)	compression ratio	maximum power (hp)	rpm (engine)	number and type of carburetors
27	51	212 Export	12 V	68 x 58,8	0,86	213,5	2562,6	8	150	6500	3 - 32 DCF
28	51	342 America	12 V	80 x 68	0,85	341,8	4101,6	8	230	6000	3 - 40 DCF
29	52	212 Export	12 V	68 x 58,8	0,86	213,5	2562,6	7,5	150	6500	1 - 36 DCF
30	52	212 Inter	12 V	68 x 58,8	0,86	213,5	2562,6	8	170	6500	3 - 36 DCF
31	52	250 Europa	12 V	68 x 68	1	246,9	2963,4	8	200	6300	3 - 36 DCF
32	52	340 Mexico	12 V	80 x 68	0,85	341,8	4101,6	8	280	6600	3 - 40 DCF
33	52	340 MM	12 V	80 x 68	0,85	341,8	4101,6	8	280	6600	3 - 40 DCF
34	52	342 America	12 V	80 x 68	0,85	341,8	4101,6	8	200	5000	3 - 40 DCF
35	52	375 Indian.	12 V	80 x 74,5	0,93	374,5	4493,7	13	384	7500	3 - 40 IF4C
36	52	250 MM	12 V	73 x 58,8	0,80	246,1	2953,2	9	240	7200	3 - 36 IF4C
37	52	500 F 2	4 L	90 x 78	0,87	496,2	1984,9	12	180	7200	2 - 50 DCO
38	52	225 S	12 V	70 x 58,8	0,84	226,3	2715,4	8,5	210	7200	3 - 36 DCF
39	52	735 S	4 L	102 x 90	0,88	735,4	2941,6	9	225	6800	2 - 50 DCOA
40	53	212 Inter	12 V	68 x 58,8	0,86	213,5	2562,6	8	170	6500	3 - 36 DCF
41	53	250 Europa	12 V	73 x 58,8	0,80	246,1	2953,2	9	240	7000	3 - 36 DCF
42	53	275 MM	12 V	72 x 68	0,94	276,8	3322,3	8,5	270	7000	3 - 40 DCF
43	53	375 MM	12 V	84 x 68	0,81	376,8	4522,9	9	340	7000	3 - 40 IF4C
44	53	375 America	12 V	84 x 68	0,81	376,8	4522,9	8	300	6300	3 - 40 DCF
45	53	553 F 2	4 L	93 x 73,5	0,79	499,3	1997,2	13	190	7500	2 - 50 DCO
46	53	340 Mexico	12 V	80 x 68	0,85	341,8	4101,6	8,5	280	6600	3 - 40 DCF
47	53	625 F 1	4 L	94 x 90	0,96	624,6	2498,3	13	240	7000	2 - 50 DCOA
48	53	700	4 L	99 x 90	0,91	692,8	2771,2	12	250	6800	2 - 45 DCOA
49	54	250 Europa	12 V	73 x 58,8	0,80	246,1	2953,2	8,5	220	7000	3 - 36 DCF
50	54	500 Mondial	4 L	90 x 78	0,87	496,2	1984,8	8,2	170	7000	2 - 45 DCO A/3
51	54	750 Monza	4 L	103 x 90	0,87	749,9	2999,6	9,2	250	6000	2 - 58 DCO A/3
52	54	625 F 1	4 L	94 x 90	0,95	624,6	2498,4	12	240	7000	2 - 50 DCOA
53	54	555 F 1	4 L	100 x 79,5	0,79	624,4	2497,6	12	250	7500	2 - 52 DCOA
54	54	625 Mondial	4 L	94 x 90	0,95	624,6	2498,4	9,2	220	6800	2 - 46 DCOA
55	54	375 Plus	12 V	84 x 74,5	0,88	412,8	4954,4	9,2	344	6500	3 - 46 DCF
56	54	275 Speciale	12 V	88 x 68	0,77	413,6	4962,8	9	380	7000	3 - 46 DCF
57	54	375 S coupé America	12 V	84 x 68	0,81	376,8	4522,9	9,2	350	7000	3 - 42 DCZ
58	54	306 S	6 L	90 x 78	0,87	496,2	2977,2	8,5	240	7000	3 - 40 DCO
59	55	555 F 1	4 L	100 x 79,5	0,79	624,4	2497,6	14	270	7500	2 - 52 DCOA
60	55	(115) 256 F 1	6 L	82,4 x 78	0,95	416	2496	12	250	6500	3 - 45 DCOA
61	55	(116) 252 F 1	2 L	118 x 114	0,96	1246,7	2493,4	13	174	4800	2 - 42 DCOD
62	55	(118) 376 LM	6 L	94 x 90	0,95	624,6	3747,6	9	310	6000	3 - 45 DCOA
63	55	250 GT	12 V	73 x 58,8	0,80	246,1	2953,2	8,5	220	7000	3 - 36 DCF
64	55	500 Mondial	4 L	90 x 78	0,87	496,2	1984,8	8,5	170	7000	2 - 40 DCO A/3
65	55	625 Mondial	4 L	94 x 90	0,95	624,6	2498,4	9,2	220	6800	2 - 46 DCOA
66	55	750 Monza	4 L	103 x 90	0,87	749,9	2999,6	8,6	260	6000	2 - 52 DCOA
67	55	410 SA	12 V	88 x 68	0,77	413,6	4962,8	8,5	340	6000	3 - 40 DCF
68	55	(121) 446 S	6 L	102 x 90	0,88	735,4	4412,5	8,5	330	6000	3 - 50 DCOA
69	55	(123)	6 L	100 x 90	0,90	706,8	4241,1	9	330	6000	

Ignition: S = simple; D = double: B = reel; M = magneto. Engine position: A = Front; P = rear. Gearbox position: A = front; P = rear; V = overdrive. Suspension: B = springs; BT = transverse springs; M = coil springs; DD = De Dion bridge; O = swinging semiaxle; I = independent or transverse parallelogram; N = normal rigid bridge.

number of camshafts	engine position	gearbox position and number of speeds	wheelbase (mm)	front track (mm)	rear track (mm)	front suspensions	rear suspensions	front tires	rear tires	weight (kg)	capacity fuel tank (l)	maximum speed (kph)
B	1	A 5	2250	1270	1250	I-BT	N-B	5,90 x 15	5,90 x 15	800	120	220
B	1	A 5	2420	1278	1250	I-BT	N-B	6,40 x 15	6,40 x 15	900	135	240
B	1	A 5	2600	1278	1250	I-BT	N-B	6,40 x 15	6,40 x 15	1000	105	196
B	1	A 5	2250	1278	1250	I-BT	N-B	5,50 x 16	6,50 x 16	850	120	220
B	1	A 4	2800	1325	1320	I-BT	N-B	7,10 x 15	7,10 x 15	1150	140	218
B	1	A 5	2600	1278	1250	I-BT	N-B	6,00 x 16	6,50 x 16	900	150	280
B	1	A 5	2500	1325	1320	I-BT	N-B	6,00 x 16	6,50 x 16	850	150	270
B	1	A 4	2650	1325	1320	I-BT	N-B	6,40 x 15	6,40 x 15	1200	105	186
4 M	1	P 4	2350	1270	1250	I-M	DD-BT	6,00 x 16	8,00 x 18	750	180	325
B	1	A 4	2400	1300	1320	I-BT	N-B	5,50 x 16	6,00 x 16	850	150	250
2 M	2	P 4	2160	1270	1250	I-BT	DD-BT	5,25 x 16	6,50 x 16	560	150	240
B	1	A 5	2250	1278	1250	I-BT	N-B	6,00 x 16	6,00 x 16	850	120	230
2 B	2	Experimental engine										
B	1	A 5	2600	1278	1250	I-BT	N-B	6,40 x 15	6,40 x 15	1000	105	200
B	1	A 4	2800	1325	1320	I-BT	N-B	7,10 x 15	7,10 x 15	1150	140	218
M	1	A 4	2500	1325	1320	I-BT	N-B	6,00 x 16	7,00 x 16	860	150	250
M	1	A 4	2600	1325	1320	I-BT	N-B	6,00 x 16	7,00 x 16	900	180	290
B	1	A 4	2800	1325	1320	I-BT	N-B	7,10 x 15	7,10 x 15	1150	140	250
2 M	2	P 4	2160	1270	1250	I-BT	DD-BT	5,25 x 16	6,50 x 16	560	150	260
2 B	1	A 5	2600	1278	1250	I-BT	N-B	6,00 x 16	6,50 x 16	900	150	230
2 M	2	Experimental engine										
2 M	2	Experimental engine										
B	1	A 4	2600	1354	1349	I-BT	N-B	6,00 x 16	6,00 x 16	1050	100	218
2 M	2	P 5	2250	1278	1284	I-BT	DD-BT	5,25 x 16	6,00 x 16	720	145	236
2 M	2	P 5	2250	1278	1284	I-BT	DD-BT	5,25 x 16	6,00 x 16	760	150	264
2 M	2	P 4	2160	1278	1250	I-BT	DD-BT	5,25 x 16	7,00 x 16	600	180	250
2 M	2	P 4	2160	1278	1250	I-M	DD-BT	5,25 x 16	7,00 x 16	590	180	250
2 M	2	P 4	2250	1278	1284	I-BT	DD-BT	5,25 x 16	6,00 x 16	730	120	240
M	1	P 4	2600	1325	1284	I-BT	DD-BT	6,00 x 16	7,00 x 16	900	150	270
4 B	1	P 4	2350	1316	1286	I-M	DD-BT	6,00 x 16	7,00 x 16	950	140	280
M	1	A 4	2600	1325	1320	I-BT	N-B	6,00 x 16	6,00 x 16	1100	140	250
2 M	2	P 4	2480	1278	1284	I-M	DD-BT	5,25 x 16	6,00 x 16	850	150	240
2 M	2	P 4	2160	1270	1250	I-M	DD-BT	5,25 x 16	7,00 x 16	590	180	270
2 M	2	Experimental engine										
2 M	2	Experimental engine										
2 B	2	P 5	2400	1216	1284	I-M	DD-BT	6,00 x 16	7,50 x 16	850	150	260
B	1	A 4	2600	1354	1350	I-M	N-B	6,00 x 16	6,00 x 16	1050	100	220
2 B	2	P 5	2250	1278	1284	I-M	DD-BT	5,25 x 16	6,00 x 16	720	150	236
2 B	2	P 5	2250	1278	1284	I-M	DD-BT	5,25 x 16	6,00 x 16	720	150	240
2 B	2	P 5	2250	1278	1284	I-M	DD-BT	5,25 x 16	6,00 x 16	760	150	264
2 B	1	A 4	2800	1455	1450	I-M	N-B	6,50 x 16	6,50 x 16	1200	100	260
2 B	2	P 5	2400	1278	1284	I-M	DD-BT	6,00 x 16	7,00 x 16	900	150	260
		Experimental engine										

number	year	model	number of cylinders	bore and stroke (mm)	stroke/bore	ind. cylinder displacement (cm³)	total displacement (cm³)	compression ratio	maximum power (hp)	rpm (engine)	number and type of carburetors
70	·55	(124)	4 L	110 x 90	0,82	855,3	3421,2				
71	55	(127)	6 L	97,5 x 78	0,80	582,3	3494,2				
72	55	250 compress.	12 V	68 x 68	1	246,9	2963,5	6	510	7000	1 - 40 IF4C
73	55	857 S	4 L	102 x 105	1,03	857,9	3431,9	8,5	280	5800	2 - 58 DCOA
74	56	625 F I	4 L	94 x 90	0,95	624,6	2498,4	12	250	7500	2 - 50 DCOA
75	56	050/555 F I Squalo	8 V	76 x 68,8	0,90	312,1	2496,8	12	231	8600	4 - 40 DCS
76	56	500 TR	4 L	90 x 78	0,87	496,2	1984,9	8,5	180	7000	2 - 40 DCO
77	56	250 GI	12 V	73 x 58,8	0,80	246,1	2953,2	8,5	240	7000	3 - 36 DCF
78	56	410 SA	12 V	88 x 68	0,77	413,6	4962,8	8,5	340	6000	3 - 42 DCF
79	56	290 MM	12 V	73 x 69,5	0,95	290,8	3490,3	9	320	6800	3 - 46 TRA
80	56	625 LM	4 L	94 x 90	0,95	624,6	2498,4	9	225	6200	2 - 42 DCOA
81	56	860 Monza	4 L	102 x 105	1,03	857,9	3431,9	9	310	6200	2 - 58 DCOA
82	56	446 Indian.	6 L	102 x 90	0,88	735,4	4412,5	9	360	6300	3 - 50 DCOA
83	56	500/750	4 L	100 x 95	0,95	746,1	2984,5	8,6	260	6000	2 - 52 DCO
84	56	750/625	4 L	103 x 90	0,87	749,9	2999,6	9,5	280	6500	2 - 50 DCOA
85	56	860/555	4 L	102 x 105	1,03	857,9	3431,9	9,5	310	6200	2 - 58 DCOA
86	56	(128) 260	12 V	75 x 58,8	0,78	259,8	3117,2				
87	56	V8 Sperim.	8 V	74 x 72,2	0,98	310,5	2484,2	12			
88	57	801 F I	8 V	80 x 62	0,78	311,8	2494,8	11	285	8800	4 - 40 DCS
89	57	156 F 2	6 V	70 x 64,5	0,92	248,2	1489,3	10	180	9000	3 - 38 DCN
90	57	156 S	6 V	70 x 64,5	0,92	248,2	1489,3	9,2	170	8500	3 - 36 DCN
91	57	410 SA	12 V	88 x 68	0,77	413,6	4962,8	8,5	340	6000	3 - 42 DCF
92	57	250 GT	12 V	73 x 58,8	0,80	246,1	2953,2	8,5	240	7000	3 - 36 DCF
93	57	500 TRC	4 L	90 x 78	0,87	496,2	1984,9	8,75	190	7500	2 - 40 DCO
94	57	290 S	12 V	73 x 69,5	0,95	290,8	3490,3	9	350	7200	6 - 42 DCN
95	57	315 S	12 V	76 x 69,5	0,91	315,3	3783,5	9	360	7200	6 - 42 DCN
96	57	335 S	12 V	77 x 72	0,93	335,3	4023,3	9,2	390	7800	6 - 42 DCN
97	57	(139) 298 S	8 V	81 x 72,8	0,90	375,1	3000,8	11,5			4 - Solex 40 PJ
98	57	196 S	6 V	77 x 71	0,92	330,6	1983,7	10	225	8600	3 - 42 DCN
99	57	226 S	6 V	81 x 71	0,88	365,8	2195,2	10	235	8000	3 - 42 DCN
100	58	246 F I	6 V	85 x 71	0,83	402,9	2417,3	11	270	8300	3 - 42 DCN
101	58	(326) 528 MI	6 V	87 x 90	1,04	535	3210,1	9	330	7500	3 - 54 DCN
102	58	(412) 530 MI	12 V	77 x 72	0,93	335,3	4023,3	9,4	415	8500	6 - 42 DCN
103	58	250 GT	12 V	73 x 58,8	0,80	246,1	2953,2	8,5	240	7000	3 - 36 DCF
104	58	250 TRS	12 V	73 x 58,8	0,80	246,1	2953,2	9,8	300	7200	6 - 40 DCN
105	58	196 S (Dino)	6 V	77 x 71	0,92	330,6	1983,7	9,8	195	7800	3 - 42 DCN
106	58	296 S (Dino)	6 V	85 x 87	1,02	493,7	2962,1	9	300	8000	3 - 46 DCN
107	58	312 LM	12 V	73 x 58,8	0,80	246,1	2953,2	10	280	8500	6 - 42 DCN
108	58	410 SA	12 V	88 x 68	0,77	413,6	4962,8	8,5	340	6000	3 - 42 DCF
109	58	196 GT	6 V	77 x 71	0,92	330,6	1983,7	9	175	7500	3 - 38 DCN
110	58	(144)	12 V	75 x 65	0,87	287,1	3445,9	9			
111	58	256 F I	6 V	86 x 71	0,82	412,4	2474,5	9,8	290	8800	3 - 42 DCN
112	58	(152)	6 V	84 x 72	0,87	399	2394	9			3 - 42 DCN
113	58	(153) 156 S	6 V	72 x 64,5	0,90	262,6	1575,6	9	165	8000	3 - 38 DCN
114	59	256 F I	6 V	86 x 71	0,83	412,4	2474,6	10	280	8500	3 - 42 DCN

Ignition: S = simple; D = double; B = reel; M = magneto. **Engine position:** A = Front; P = rear. **Gearbox position:** A = front; P = rear; V = overdrive. **Suspension:** B = springs; BT = transverse springs; M = coil springs; DD = De Dion bridge; O = swinging semiaxle; I = independent or transverse parallelogram; N = normal rigid bridge.

ignition	number of camshafts	engine position	gearbox position and number of speeds	wheelbase (mm)	front track (mm)	rear track (mm)	front suspensions	rear suspensions	front tires	rear tires	weight (kg)	capacity fuel tank (l)	maximum speed (kph)
		Experimental engine											
		Experimental engine											
4 M	2	Experimental engine											
2 M	2	A	P 4	2300	1378	1284	I-M	DD-BT	6,50 x 16	6,50 x 16	860	165	260
2 M	2	A	P 5	2160	1270	1250	I-M	DD-BT	5,25 x 16	7,00 x 16	620	150	250
2 M	2	A	P 5	2160	1270	1250	I-M	DD-BT	5,25 x 16	7,00 x 16	630	150	250
2 B	2	A	A 4	2250	1308	1250	I-M	N-M	5,50 x 16	6,00 x 16	680	120	245
2 B	1	A	A 4	2600	1354	1350	I-M	N-B	6,00 x 16	6,00 x 16	1050	100	250
2 B	1	A	A 4	2800	1455	1450	I-M	N-B	6,50 x 16	6,50 x 16	1200	100	260
4 B	1	A	P 4	2350	1310	1286	I-M	DD-BT	6,00 x 16	7,00 x 16	880	190	280
2 B	2	A	A 4	2250	1308	1250	I-M	N-M	5,50 x 16	6,00 x 16	700	130	250
2 M	2	A	P 4	2350	1308	1280	I-M	DD-BT	6,00 x 16	7,00 x 16	860	165	260
2 M	2	Kurtis Kraft chassis											
2 B	2	A	A 4	2250	1308	1300	I-M	N-M	5,50 x 16	6,00 x 16	700	90	
2 M	2	A	P 4	2160	1270	1250	I-B	DD-B	5,25 x 16	7,00 x 16	650	150	260
2 M	2	A	P 4	2160	1270	1250	I-M	DD-B	5,25 x 16	7,00 x 16	650	150	
		Experimental engine											
		Experimental engine											
2 M	2	A	P 5	2280	1320	1270	I-M	DD-BT	5,50 x 16	7,00 x 16	650	170	270
1 M	2	A	P 5	2160	1270	1250	I-M	DD-BT	5,50 x 15	6,50 x 16	512	150	240
2 B	2	A	A 4	2220	1240	1200	I-M	N-M	5,50 x 15	6,50 x 16	520	150	220
2 B	1	A	A 4	2800	1455	1450	I-M	N-B	6,50 x 16	6,50 x 16	1200	100	260
2 B	1	A	A 4	2600	1354	1350	I-M	N-B	6,00 x 16	6,00 x 16	1050	100	250
2 B	2	A	A 4	2250	1308	1250	I-M	N-M	5,50 x 16	6,00 x 16	680	150	260
4 B	2	A	P 4	2350	1310	1286	I-M	DD-BT	6,00 x 16	7,00 x 16	880	190	290
4 B	1	A	P 4	2350	1310	1286	I-M	DD-BT	6,00 x 16	7,00 x 16	880	190	290
4 B	1	A	P 4	2350	1310	1286	I-M	DD-BT	6,00 x 16	7,00 x 16	880	190	300
		Experimental engine											
1 M	2	Experimental engine											
1 M	2	Experimental engine											
1 M	2	A	P 4	2220	1240	1240	I-M	DD-BT	5,50 x 16	6,50 x 16	560	160	270
2 B	2	A	P 3	2220	1240	1240	I-M	DD-M	6,00 x 16	8,00 x 16	660	166	300
4 M	2	A	P 3	2300	1296	1310	I-M	DD-M	6,70 x 16	8,00 x 18	700	204	300
2 B	1	A	A 4	2600	1354	1350	I-M	N-B	6,00 x 16	6,00 x 16	1200	100	240
4 B	1	A	A 4	2350	1310	1300	I-M	N-M	5,50 x 16	6,00 x 16	800	180	270
2 B	1	A	A 4	2200	1240	1200	I-M	N-M	5,50 x 16	6,00 x 16	680	150	240
2 B	2	Experimental engine											
4 B	2	A	P 4	2350	1310	1300	I-M	DD-BT	6,00 x 16	7,00 x 16	800	180	290
2 B	1	A	A 4	2800	1455	1450	I-M	N-B	6,50 x 16	6,50 x 16	1200	100	260
1 B	1	Experimental engine											
		Experimental engine											
2 B	2	Experimental engine											
		Experimental engine											
1 B	1	Experimental engine											
1 M	2	A	P 4	2220	1240	1240	I-M	DD-BT	5,50 x 16	6,50 x 16	560	150	270

number	year	model	number of cylinders	bore and stroke (mm)	stroke/bore	ind. cylinder displacement (cm³)	total displacement (cm³)	compression ratio	maximum power (hp)	rpm (engine)	number and type of carburetors
115	59	250 TRS	12 V	73 x 58,8	0,80	246,1	2953,2	9,8	300	7200	6 - 40 DCN
116	59	250 GT	12 V	73 x 58,8	0,80	246,1	2953,2	8,5	240	7000	3 - 36 DCF
117	59	410 SA	12 V	88 x 68	0,77	413,6	4962,8	9	400	6500	3 - 42 DCF
118	59	410 SF	12 V	88 x 68	0,77	413,6	4962,8	9	400	6500	3 - 42 DCF
119	59	(154 S) 1500 Sport	6 V	72 x 61	0,85	248,3	1489,9	9,6	150	7000	
120	59	(155)	6 V	85 x 72	0,85	408,5	2451,1	9,8			
121	59	(159)	12 V	77 x 75	0,98	349,2	4190,4	9			
122	59	(161) 854	4 L	65 x 64	0,98	212,3	849,5	7,5	68	7000	2 - 38 DCO
123	59	(162) F. Interc.	12 V	75 x 71	0,95	313,6	3764				
124	59	(163) 330 GT	12 V	77 x 71	0,92	330,6	3967,4	9,8	380	7000	6 - 40 DCN
125	59	(164) 950°	4 L	67 x 69	1,03	243,2	973	9	80	7000	2 - 32 DCN
126	59	850 coupé	4 L	65 x 64	0,98	212,3	849,5	9	86	7000	2 - 38 DCO
127	59	156 F 2	6 V	73 x 58,8	0,80	246,1	1476,6	9,2	150	8000	3 - 38 DCN
128	60	246 - F I Long chassis	6 V	85 x 71	0,83	402,9	2417,3	9,8	280	8500	3 - 42 DCN
129	60	246 - F I Short chassis	6 V	85 x 71	0,83	402,9	2417,3	9,8	280	8500	3 - 42 DCN
130	60	256 - F I Single camshaft	6 V	85 x 71	0,83	402,9	2417,3	9,8	250	7700	3 - 42 DCN
131	60	296 F L	6 V	87 x 83	0,95	493,4	2960,6	9,9	298	8200	3 - 42 DCN
132	60	250 TRS	12 V	73 x 58,8	0,80	246,1	2953,2	9,3	300	7500	6 - 42 DCN
133	60	250 Injection	12 V	73 x 58,8	0,80	246,1	2953,2	9,2	300	7500	Bosch Inj.
134	60	246 Injection	6 V	85 x 71	0,83	402,9	2417,3	9,8	280	8500	Bosch Inj.
135	60	250 GT coupé-cabriolet	12 V	73 x 58,8	0,80	246,1	2953,2	8,5	240	7000	3 - 36 DCF
136	60	250 GT spider	12 V	73 x 58,8	0,80	246,1	2953,2	9	280	7500	3 - 36 DCF
137	60	400 SA	12 V	77 x 71	0,92	330,6	3967,4	9	400	7000	3 - 46 DCF
138	60	F 1 - Rear	6 V	86,4 x 71	0,82	416,3	2497,6	11	245	7600	3 - 42 DCN
139	60	F 2 - Front	6 V	73 x 59,1	0,80	247,3	1484	9,8	180	9000	3 - 38 DCW
140	60	F 2 - Rear	6 V	73 x 59,1	0,80	247,3	1484	9,8	180	9000	3 - 38 DCW
141	60	(164 bis) 1000	4 L	69 x 69	1	258	1032	9	100	7200	2 - 38 DCOA
142	60	(165) 1600 GT	6 V	73 x 62	0,85	259,5	1556,8	9,8	160	7500	3 - 42 DCN
143	61	156 F I - 65°	6 V	73 x 59	0,80	246,9	1481,4	9,8	180	9000	3 - 38 DCW
144	61	156 F I - 65°	6 V	67 x 70	1,04	246,8	1480,7	9,8	185	9500	3 - 42 DCN
145	61	156 F I - 65°	6 V	81 x 48,2	0,60	249,4	1496,4	9,8	200	10.500	3 - 42 DCN
146	61	156 F I - 120°	6 V	73 x 58,8	0,80	246,1	1476,6	9,8	190	9500	2 - 40 IF3C
147	61	250 S	12 V	73 x 58,8	0,80	246,1	2953,2	9,8	300	7500	6 - 42 DCN
148	61	276 S	6 V	90 x 71	0,79	451,7	2710,2	9,9	275	7700	3 - 42 DCN
149	61	250 GT 2+2	12 V	73 x 58,8	0,80	246,1	2953,2	8,5	240	7000	3 - 36 DCF
150	61	250 coupé cabriolet	12 V	73 x 58,8	0,80	246,1	2953,2	8,5	240	7000	3 - 36 DCF
151	61	250 berlinetta spider	12 V	73 x 58,8	0,80	246,1	2953,2	9	280	7500	3 - 36 DCF
152	61	400 SA	12 V	77 x 71	0,92	330,6	3967,4	9	400	7000	3 - 46 DCF
153	61	246 P	6 V	85 x 71	0,83	402,9	2417,3	9,8	270	8000	3 - 42 DCN
154	61	296 S	6 V	87 x 82	0,94	487,5	2924,9	9,8	310	7500	
155	62	F I - 120°	6 V	73 x 58,8	0,80	246,1	1476,6	9,8	200	10.000	2 - 40 IF3C

Ignition: S = simple; D = double: B = reel; M = magneto. **Engine position:** A = Front; P = rear. **Gearbox position:** A = front; P = rear; V = overdrive. **Suspension:** B = springs; BT = transverse springs; M = coil springs; DD = De Dion bridge; O = swinging semiaxle; I = independent or transverse parallelogram; N = normal rigid bridge.

ignition	number of camshafts	engine position	gearbox position and number of speeds	wheelbase (mm)	front track (mm)	rear track (mm)	front suspensions	rear suspensions	front tires	rear tires	weight (kg)	capacity fuel tank (l)	maximum speed (kph)
S 2 B	1	A	A 4	2350	1310	1300	I-M	N-M	5,50 x 16	6,00 x 16	800	180	270
S 2 B	1	A	A 4	2600	1354	1350	I-M	N-B	6,00 x 16	6,00 x 16	1200	100	240
S 2 B	1	A	A 4	2800	1455	1450	I-M	N-B	6,50 x 16	6,50 x 16	1320	100	260
S 2 B	1	A	A 4	2600	1354	1350	I-M	N-B	6,50 x 16	6,50 x 16	1100	100	280
		Experimental engine											
		Experimental engine											
		Experimental engine											
S 1 B	1	Experimental engine											
		Experimental engine											
S 2 B	2	Experimental engine											
S 1 B	1	Experimental engine											
S 1 B	1	A	A 4 V	2200	1280	1280	I-M	N-B	135 x 13	135 x 13	680	55	160
S 1 B	1	Experimental engine											
D 1 M	2	A	P 5	2320	1240	1300	I-M	I-M	5,50 x 15	6,50 x 16	560	150	270
D 1 M	2	A	P 5	2220	1240	1300	I-M	I-M	5,50 x 15	6,50 x 16	560	150	270
D 1 M	1	A	P 5	2220	1240	1300	I-M	I-M	5,50 x 15	6,50 x 16	540	140	260
D 1 M	2	A	P 5	2320	1240	1300	I-M	I-M	5,50 x 16	7,00 x 16	560	150	270
S 2 B	1	A	A 5	2280	1225	1260	I-M	DD-M	5,50 x 16	6,50 x 16	800	120	270
S 2 B	1	Experimental engine											
D 2 B	2	Experimental engine											
S 2 B	1	A	A 4 V	2600	1354	1350	I-M	N-B	6,00 x 16	6,00 x 16	1200	120	240
S 2 B	1	A	A 4	2420	1354	1350	I-M	N-B	6,00 x 16	6,00 x 16	960	120	260
S 2 B	1	A	A 4 V	2450	1359	1350	I-M	N-B	6,50 x 15	6,70 x 15	1250	120	280
S 1 M	2	P	P 5	2300	1200	1200	I-M	I-M	5,25 x 15	6,50 x 15	550	152	260
D 1 M	2	A	P 5	2220	1240	1300	I-M	I-M	5,25 x 15	6,00 x 15	490	150	230
D 1 M	2	P	P 5	2300	1200	1200	I-M	I-M	5,25 x 15	6,00 x 15	470	105	230
S 1 B	1	Experimental engine											
S 1 B	1	Experimental engine											
D 1 M	2	P	P 5	2300	1200	1200	I-M	I-M	5,25 x 15	6,00 x 15	460	105	240
D 1 M	2	Experimental engine											
D 1 M	2	Experimental engine											
D 1 M	2	P	P 5	2300	1200	1200	I-M	I-M	5,00 x 15	6,00 x 15	460	130	240
S 2 B	1	A	P 5	2350	1225	1260	I-M	I-M	5,50 x 16	6,50 x 16	770	130	270
S 1 M	1	Experimental engine											
S 2 B	1	A	A 4 V	2600	1354	1350	I-M	N-B	6,00 x 16	6,00 x 16	1280	120	240
S 2 B	1	A	A 4 V	2600	1354	1350	I-M	N-B	6,00 x 16	6,00 x 16	1200	120	240
S 2 B	1	A	A 4	2420	1354	1350	I-M	N-B	6,00 x 16	6,00 x 16	960	120	270
S 2 B	1	A	A 4 V	2420	1359	1350	I-M	N-B	6,50 x 15	6,50 x 15	1280	120	280
D 2 B	2	P	P 5	2320	1310	1300	I-M	I-M	5,50 x 15	6,50 x 15	590	120	260
D 1 M	2	Experimental engine											
D 2 B	2	P	P 6	2350	1340	1320	I-M	I-M	5,00 x 15	6,50 x 15	490	120	240

number	year	model	number of cylinders	bore and stroke (mm)	stroke/bore	ind. cylinder displacement (cm³)	total displacement (cm³)	compression ratio	maximum power (hp)	rpm (engine)	number and type of carburetors
156	62	F I - 65°	6 V	67 x 70	1,04	246,8	1480,7	9,8	190	9400	3 - 40 DCN
157	62	196 Sp	6 V	77 x 71	0,92	330,6	1983,7	9,8	210	7500	3 - 42 DC
158	62	248 Sp	8 V	77 x 66	0,85	307,3	2458,4	9,8	250	7400	4 - 40 DC
159	62	286 Sp	6 V	90 x 75	0,83	477,1	2862,9	9,5	260	6800	3 - 46 DC
160	62	250 Berl.	12 V	73 x 58,8	0,80	246,1	2953,2	9,8	300	7400	6 - 42 DCN
161	62	246 Sp	6 V	85 x 71	0,83	402,9	2417,3	9,5	275	7500	3 - 42 DC
162	62	268 Sp	8 V	77 x 71	0,92	330,6	2644,9	9,6	265	7000	4 - 40 DC
163	62	330 TR	12 V	77 x 71	0,92	330,6	3967,4	8,7	390	7500	6 - 42 DCN
164	62	330 LM - B	12 V	77 x 71	0,92	330,6	3967,4	8,7	390	7500	6 - 42 DCN
165	62	400 SA	12 V	77 x 71	0,92	330,6	3967,4	8,8	340	7000	3 - 40 DCZ
166	62	250 GT 2+2	12 V	73 x 58,8	0,80	246,1	2953,2	8,5	240	7000	3 - 36 DCF
167	63	156 F I Injection 120°	6 V	73 x 58,8	0,80	246,1	1476,6	10	200	10.200	Bosch Inj.
168	63	158 F I Monocoque	8 V	67 x 52,8	0,76	186,1	1489,3	9,8	200	10.500	Bosch Inj.
169	63	156 F I Monocoque	6 V	73 x 58,8	0,80	246,1	1476,6	10	200	10.200	Bosch Inj.
170	63	186 GT	6 V	77 x 64	0,83	298	1788,1	9,2	156	7000	3 - 38 DCN
171	63	196 S	6 V	77 x 71	0,92	330,6	1983,7	9	200	7500	3 - 42 DCN
172	63	250 P	12 V	73 x 58,8	0,80	246,1	2953,2	9,5	310	7500	6 - 38 DCN
173	63	330 LM	12 V	77 x 71	0,92	330,6	3967,4	9	400	7500	6 - 42 DCN
174	63	250 GT - 2+2	12 V	73 x 58,8	0,80	246,1	2953,2	9,2	240	7000	3 - 36 DCF
175	63	250 GTO e spider	12 V	73 x 58,8	0,80	246,1	2953,2	9,2	250	7500	6 - 38 DCN
176	63	400 SA	12 V	77 x 71	0,92	330,6	3967,4	8,8	340	7000	3 - 40 DCZ
177	64	158 F I	8 V	67 x 52,8	0,76	186,1	1489,3	9,8	200	10.500	Bosch Inj.
178	64	512 F I	12 C	56 x 50,4	0,90	124,1	1489,6	9,8	220	12.000	Lucas Inj.
179	64	500 SF	12 V	88 x 68	0,77	413,6	4962,8	8,8	400	6500	3 - 40 DCZ6
180	64	330 GT - 2+2	12 V	77 x 71	0,92	330,6	3967,4	8,8	300	6600	3 - 40 DCZ6
181	64	365 P	12 V	81 x 71	0,87	365,8	4390,3	9,5	380	7200	6 - 38 DCN
182	64	330 P	12 V	77 x 71	0,92	330,6	3967,4	9	390	7500	6 - 42 DCN
183	64	275 P	12 V	77 x 58,8	0,76	273,8	3285,7	9,8	320	7700	6 - 38 DCN
184	64	250 LM	12 V	73 x 58,8	0,80	246,1	2953,2	9,7	300	7500	6 - 38 DCN
185	64	275 GTB	12 V	77 x 58,8	0,76	273,8	3285,7	9,2	280	7500	3 6 } 40 DCZ6
186	64	275 GTS	12 V	77 x 58,8	0,76	273,8	3285,7	9,2	260	7000	3 - 40 DCZ6
187	64	250 GTO/64	12 V	73 x 58,8	0,80	246,1	2953,2	9,8	300	7700	6 - 38 DCN
188	65	275 P 2	12 V	77 x 58,8	0,76	273,8	3285,7	9,8	350	8500	6 - 40 DCN/2
189	65	330 P 2	12 V	77 x 71	0,92	330,6	3967,4	9,8	410	8200	6 - 42 DCN/2
190	65	166 Dino	6 V	77 x 57	0,74	265,4	1592,7	9,8	180	9000	3 - 40 DCN
191	65	206 Sp (Dino)	6 V	86 x 57	0,66	331,1	1986,7	{ 12,5 9,8	218	9000	3 - 40 DCN/2
192	65	158 F I	8 V	67 x 52,8	0,76	186,1	1489,3	9,8	210	11.000	Bosch Inj.
193	65	512 F I	12 C	56 x 50,4	0,90	124,1	1489,6	9,8	220	12.000	Lucas Inj.
194	65	330 GT - 2+2	12 V	77 x 71	0,92	330,6	3967,4	8,8	300	6600	3 - 40 DCZ6
195	65	500 SF	12 V	88 x 68	0,77	413,6	4962,8	8,8	400	6500	3 - 40 DCZ6
196	65	275 GTB	12 V	77 x 58,8	0,76	273,8	3285,7	9,5	280	7600	3 6 } 40 DCZ6

Ignition: S = simple; D = double; B = reel; M = magneto. **Engine position:** A = Front; P = rear. **Gearbox position:** A = front; P = rear; V = overdrive. **Suspension:** B = springs; BT = transverse springs; M = coil springs; DD = De Dion bridge; O = swinging semiaxle; I = independent or transverse parallelogram; N = normal rigid bridge.

ignition	number of camshafts	engine position	gearbox position and number of speeds	wheelbase (mm)	front track (mm)	rear track (mm)	front suspensions	rear suspensions	front tires	rear tires	weight (kg)	capacity fuel tank (l)	maximum speed (kph)
D 2 B	2	P	P 6	2320	1200	1200	I-M	I-M	5,00 x 15	6,50 x 15	470	120	240
S 1 B	1	P	P 5	2320	1310	1300	I-M	I-M	5,25 x 15	6,50 x 15	600	100	240
S 2 B	1	P	P 5	2320	1310	1300	I-M	I-M	5,25 x 15	6,50 x 15	640	120	250
S 1 B	1	P	P 5	2320	1310	1300	I-M	I-M	5,25 x 15	7,00 x 15	620	120	250
S 2 B	1	A	A 5	2400	1354	1350	I-M	N-M	6,00 x 15	7,00 x 15	930	130	270
D 2 B	2	P	P 5	2320	1310	1300	I-M	I-M	5,50 x 15	7,00 x 15	750	118	270
S 2 B	1	P	P 5	2320	1310	1300	I-M	I-M	5,50 x 15	7,00 x 15	770	125	260
S 2 B	1	A	A 5	2420	1354	1350	I-M	I-M	6,00 x 16	7,00 x 16	877	136	300
S 2 B	1	A	A 4	2420	1354	1350	I-M	I-M	6,00 x 15	7,00 x 15	1046	136	300
S 2 B	1	A	A 4 V	2600	1395	1387	I-M	N-B	205 x 15	205 x 15	1280	100	265
S 2 B	1	A	A 4 V	2600	1354	1350	I-M	N-B	6,00 x 16	6,00 x 16	1280	120	240
D 2 B	2	P	P 6	2380	1330	1380	I-M	I-M	5,50 x 15	6,50 x 15	470	120	260
D 4 B	2	P	P 6	2380	1350	1340	I-M	I-M	5,50 x 15	6,50 x 15	460	125	260
D 2 B	2	P	P 6	2380	1350	1340	I-M	I-M	5,50 x 15	6,50 x 15	460	125	260
S 1 B	1	Experimental engine											
S 1 B	2	P	P 5	2320	1310	1300	I-M	I-M	5,25 x 15	6,50 x 15	600	100	240
S 2 B	1	P	P 5	2400	1350	1340	I-M	I-M	5,50 x 15	7,00 x 15	930	124	275
S 2 B	1	A	A 5	2500	1422	1414	I-M	N-B	6,00 x 15	7,00 x 15	1000	122	280
S 2 B	1	A	A 4 V	2600	1354	1350	I-M	N-B	185 x 15	185 x 15	1300	120	230
S 2 B	1	A	A 4	2400	1354	1350	I-M	N-M	185 x 15	185 x 15	1060	130	240
S 2 B	1	A	A 4 V	2600	1395	1387	I-M	N-B-M	205 x 15	105 x 15	1300	120	265
D 4 B	2	P	P 5	2380	1369	1350	I-M	I-M	5,50 x 13	7,00 x 13	460	125	260
S 2 B	2	P	P 5	2400	1369	1350	I-M	I-M	5,50 x 13	7,00 x 13	465	128	260
S 2 B	1	A	A 4 V	2650	1397	1389	I-M	N-B	205 x 15	205 x 15	1400	100	280
S 2 B	1	A	A 4 V	2650	1397	1389	I-M	N-B	205 x 15	205 x 15	1380	90	240
S 2 B	1	P	P 5	2400	1400	1370	I-M	I-M	5,50 x 15	6,50 x 15	860	140	300
S 2 B	1	P	P 5	2400	1350	1340	I-M	I-M	5,50 x 15	7,00 x 15	880	140	300
S 2 B	1	P	P 5	2400	1350	1340	I-M	I-M	5,50 x 15	7,00 x 15	860	140	300
S 2 B	1	P	P 5	2400	1350	1340	I-M	I-M	5,50 x 15	7,00 x 15	850	130	290
S 2 B	1	A	P 5	2400	1377	1393	I-M	I-M	205 x 14	205 x 14	1100	140	270
S 2 B	1	A	P 5	2400	1377	1393	I-M	I-M	195 x 14	195 x 14	1150	100	240
S 2 B	1	A	P 5	2400	1377	1426	I-M	I-M	5,50 x 15	7,00 x 15	880	130	260
D 4 B	2	P	P 5	2400	1350	1340	I-M	I-M	5,50 x 15	7,00 x 15	875	140	300
D 4 B	2	P	P 5	2400	1350	1340	I-M	I-M	5,50 x 15	7,00 x 15	820	140	320
D 2 B	2	P	P 5	2280	1348	1355	I-M	I-M	5,50 x 13	6,50 x 13	590	100	240
D 2 B	2	P	P 5	2280	1348	1355	I-M	I-M	5,50 x 13	7,00 x 13	530	110	260
D 4 B	2	P	P 5	2380	1369	1350	I-M	I-M	5,50 x 13	7,00 x 13	460	125	260
D 4 B	2	P	P 5	2400	1369	1350	I-M	I-M	5,50 x 13	7,00 x 13	465	128	260
S 2 B	1	A	A 5	2650	1397	1389	I-M	N-B	205 x 15	205 x 15	1420	90	245
S 2 B	1	A	A 4 V	2650	1397	1389	I-M	N-B	205 x 15	205 x 15	1400	100	280
S 2 B	1	A	P 5	2400	1377	1426	I-M	I-M	195 x 14	195 x 14	1050	140	260

number	year	model	number of cylinders	bore and stroke (mm)	stroke/bore	ind. cylinder displacement (cm³)	total displacement (cm³)	compression ratio	maximum power (hp)	rpm (engine)	number and type of carburetors
197	65	275 GTS	12 V	77 x 58,8	0,76	273,8	3285,7	9,2	260	7000	3 - 40 DCZ6
198	65	275 LM	12 V	77 x 58,8	0,76	273,8	3285,7	9,7	320	7600	6 - 38 DCN
199	66	F 1	12 V	77 x 53,5	0,69	249,1	2989,2	11	360	10.000	Injection
200	66	330 GT	12 V	77 x 71	0,92	330,6	3967,4	8,8	300	7000	3 - 40 DCZ6
201	66	275 GTB	12 V	77 x 58,8	0,76	273,8	3285,7	9,5	280	7600	3 6 { 40 DCN3
202	66	275 GTS	12 V	77 x 58,8	0,76	273,8	3285,7	9,2	260	7000	3 - 40 DCZ6
203	66	275 LM	12 V	77 x 58,8	0,76	273,8	3285,7	9,7	320	7600	6 - 38 DCN
204	66	Dino 206/S	6 V	86 x 57	0,66	331,1	1986,7	10,8	218	9000	3 - 40 DCN2
205	66	330/P3	12 V	77 x 71	0,92	330,6	3967,4	11,4	420	8000	Lucas Inj.
206	66	330 GTC	12 V	77 x 71	0,92	330,6	3967,4	8,8	300	7000	3 - 40 DFI
207	66	500 SF	12 V	88 x 68	0,77	413,6	4962,8	8,8	400	6500	3 - 40 DCZ6
208	66	246 F 1	6 V	85 x 71	0,83	402,9	2417,3	9,5	275	8000	Lucas Inj.
209	67	F 1 - 67	12 V	77 x 53,5	0,69	249,13	2989,5	11	390	10.500	Lucas Inj.
210	67	330/P4	12 V	77 x 71	0,92	330,6	3967,4	11	450	8000	Lucas Inj.
211	67	206 Dino SP	6 V	86 x 57	0,66	331,1	1986,7	11	220	9000	Lucas Inj.
212	67	206 Dino GT	6 V	86 x 57	0,66	331,1	1986,7	9	180	8000	3 - 40 DCN
213	67	Dino F 2	6 V	86 x 45,8	0,53	266,05	1596,3	11	200	10.000	Lucas Inj.

N.B.: The Dino F 2 engine was changed later, see 1968

number	year	model	number of cylinders	bore and stroke (mm)	stroke/bore	ind. cylinder displacement (cm³)	total displacement (cm³)	compression ratio	maximum power (hp)	rpm (engine)	number and type of carburetors
214	67	330 GT 2+2	12 V	77 x 71	0,92	330,6	3967,4	8,8	300	7000	3 - 40 DCZ6
215	67	330 GTC	12 V	77 x 71	0,92	330,6	3967,4	8,8	300	7000	3 - 40 DFI
216	67	275 GTB	12 V	77 x 58,8	0,76	273,8	3285,7	9,5	280	7600	6 - 40 DCN
217	67	275 GTS	12 V	77 x 58,8	0,76	273,8	3285,7	9,2	260	7000	3 - 40 DCZ6
218	67·	CAN AM	12 V	79 x 71	0,9	348,04	4176,5	11	480	8500	Lucas Ind. Inj.
219	68	F 1/68	12 V	77 x 53,5	0,69	249,13	2989,5	11,8	408	11.000	Lucas Ind. Inj.
220	68	166 Dino F 2	6 V	79,5 x 53,5	0,67	265,6	1593,6	11,2	225	11.000	Lucas Inj.
221	68	Tasmania	6 V	90 x 63	0.7	400.8	2404.8	11.5	285	8900	Lucas Ind. Inj.
222	68	P 5/250	12 V	77 x 53,5	0,69	249,13	2989,5	11	400	9200	Lucas Inj.
223	68	330 GTB	12 V	77 x 71	0,92	330,6	3967,4				
224	68	330 GTC	12 V	77 x 71	0,92	330,6	3967,4	8,8	300	7000	3 - 40 DCN
225	68	330 GTS	12 V	77 x 71	0,92	330,6	3967,4	8;8	300	7000	3 - 40 DCN
226	68	365 GT 2+2	12 V	81 x 71	0,88	365,8	4390,3	8,8	320	6600	3 - 40 DCN
227	68	206 Dino GT	6 V	86 x 57	0,66	331,1	1986,7	9	180	8000	3 - 40 DCF
228	68	Can Am 612	12 V	92 x 78	0,85	518,46	6221,6	10,5	620	7000	Lucas Inj.
229	68	212 E Experimental	12 B	65 x 50	0,77	165,9	1990,8	11	280	11.000	Lucas Inj.
230	69	F 1/69	12 V	77 x 53,5	0,69	249,13	2989,5	11,8	436	11.000	Lucas Inj.
231	69	166 Dino F 2	6 V	79,5 x 53,5	0,67	265,6	1593,6	11,2	230	11.000	Lucas Inj.

Ignition: S = simple; D = double: B = reel; M = magneto. Engine position: A = Front; P = rear. Gearbox position: A = front; P = rear; V = overdrive. Suspension: B = springs; BT = transverse springs; M = coil springs; DD = De Dion bridge; O = swinging semiaxle; I = independent or transverse parallelogram; N = normal rigid bridge.

ignition	number of camshafts	engine position	gearbox position and number of speeds	wheelbase (mm)	front track (mm)	rear track (mm)	front suspensions	rear suspensions	front tires	rear tires	weight (kg)	capacity fuel tank (l)	maximum speed (kph)
2 B	1	A	P 5	2400	1377	1393	I-M	I-M	195 x 14	195 x 14	1120	100	240
2 B	1	P	P 5	2400	1350	1340	I-M	I-M	5,50 x 15	7,00 x 15	850	140	290
4 B	2	P	P 5	2400	1450	1436	I-M	I-M	5,50 x 14	7,00 x 14	550	160	
2 B	1	A	A 5	2650	1397	1389	I-M	N-B-M	205 x 15	205 x 15	1380	90	245
2 B	1	A	P 5	2400	1401	1417	I-M	I-M	205 x 14	205 x 14	1100	94	260
2 B	1	A	P 5	2400	1377	1393	I-M	I-M	195 x 14	195 x 14	1120	84	240
2 B	1	P	P 5	2400	1350	1340	I-M	I-M	5,50 x 15	7,00 x 15	850	140	290
1 B	2	P	P 5	2280	1360	1355	I-M	I-M	5,50 x 13	7,00 x 13	580	110	268
4 B	2	P	P 5	2400	1462	1431	I-M	I-M	5,50 x 15	7,00 x 15	720	140	310
2 B	1	A	P 5	2400	1401	1417	I-M	I-M	205 x 14	205 x 14	1300	90	245
2 B	1	A	A 5	2650	1405	1397	I-M	N-B-M	205 x 15	205 x 15	1400	100	280
4 B	2	P	P 5	2380	1369	1350	I-M	I-M	6,00 x 13	7,00 x 13	500	120	280
4 B	2	P	P 5	2400	1450	1436	I-M	I-M	5,50 x 14	7,00 x 14	530	120	
4 B	2	P	P 5	2400	1488	1450	I-M	I-M	4,75/10,30 x 15	6,00/12,30 x 15	860	135	320
2 B	2	P	P 5	2280	1360	1355	I-M	I-M	5,50 x 13	7,00 x 13	580	110	270
1 B	2	P	P 5	2280	1425	1400	I-M	I-M	185 x 14	185 x 14	900	100	235
2 B	2	P	P 5	2200	1405	1425	I-M	I-M	5,50/9,50 x 13	6,00/12,00 x 13	425	100	265
2 B	1	A	A 5	2650	1397	1389	I-M	N-B-M	205 x 15	205 x 15	1400	90	245
2 B	1	A	P 5	2400	1401	1417	I-M	I-M	205 x 14	205 x 14	1300	90	245
2 B	1	A	P 5	2400	1401	1417	I-M	I-M	205 x 14	205 x 14	1100	90	260
2 B	1	A	P 5	2400	1401	1417	I-M	I-M	205 x 14	205 x 14	1120	90	240
4 B	2	P	P 5	2400	1488	1450	I-M	I-M	4,75/10,30 x 15	6,00/12,30 x 15	700	140	315
2 B	2	P	P 5	2400	1547	1582	I-M	I-M	4.75/10,30 x 15	6,90/12,30 x 15	512	140	310
1 B	2	P	P 5	2250	1405	1435	I-M	I-M	5,00/9,50 x 13	6,00/14,00 x 13	420	120	270
2 B	2	P	P 5	2220	1405	1400	I-M	I-M	5,00/9,50 x 13	6,00/12,50 x 13	425	120	300
4 B	2	P	P 5	2380	1400	1430	I-M	I-M	10,15 x 15	12,15 x 15	664	120	300
2 B	1	A	P 5	2400	1401	1417	I-M	I-M	205 x 14	205 x 14	1300	90	242
2 B	1	A	P 5	2400	1401	1417	I-M	I-M	205 x 14	205 x 14	1200	90	242
2 B	1	A	A 5	2650	1438	1468	I-M	I-M	205 x 15	205 x 15	1480	100	245
ino ex	2	P Transverse	P 5	2280	1425	1400	I-M	I-M	185 x 14	185 x 14	900	65	235
ino ex	2	P	P 4	2450	1603,5	1590,8	I-M	I-M	4,90/13,90 x 15	6,00/15,50 x 15	700	140	340
2 B	2	P	P 5										
ino ex	2	P	P 5	2400	1550	1561	I-M	I-M	5,00/10,00 x 13	6,00/13,50 x 15	530	140	310
ino ex	2	P	P 5	2250	1405	1435	I-M	I-M	5,00/9,50 x 13	6,00/14,00 x 13	420	120	270

number	year	model	number of cylinders	bore and stroke (mm)	stroke/bore	ind. cylinder displacement (cm³)	total displacement (cm³)	compression ratio	maximum power (hp)	rpm (engine)	number and type of carburetors
232	69	246 Dino Tasmania	6 V	90 x 63	0,7	400,8	2404,8	11,5	290	9000	Lucas Inj.
233	69	312/P Sport	12 V	77 x 53,5	0,69	249,13	2989,5	11	420	9800	Lucas Inj.
234	69	365 GT 2+2	12 V	81 x 71	0,88	365,8	4390,3	8,8	320	6600	3 - 40 DCN
235	69	246 Dino GT	6 V	92,5 x 60	0,65	403,1	2418,4	9	195	7600	3 - 40 DCF
236	69	365 GTB/4	12 V	81 x 71	0,88	365,8	4390,3	8,8	352	7500	6 - 40 DCN 20
237	69	318 W	18 W	65 x 50	0,77	165,9	2986,2	11	450	12.000	Lucas Inj.
238	69	365 GTC	12 V	81 x 71	0,88	365,8	4390,3	8,8	320	6600	3 - 40 DCN
239	69	365 GTS	12 V	81 x 71	0,88	365,8	4390,3	8,8	320	6600	3 - 40 DCN
240	69	212 E	12 B	65 x 50	0,77	165,9	1990,8	11	300	11.800	Lucas Inj.
241	69	612 Can Am	12 V	92 x 78	0,85	518,46	6221,6	10,5	640	7700	Lucas Inj.
242	70	512 S	12 V	87 x 70	0,8	416	4994	11	550	8000	Lucas Inj.
243	70	312 B-F I	12 B	78,5 x 57,5	0,66	249,3	2991	11	450	12.000	Lucas Inj.
244	70	365 GT 2+2	12 V	81 x 71	0,88	365,8	4398,3	8,8	320	6600	3 - 40 DCN
245	70	365 Daytona	12 V	81 x 71	0,88	365,8	4390,3	9,3	350	7000	6 - 40 DCN
246	70	246 Dino GT	6 V	92,5 x 60	0,65	403,4	2418,4	9	195	7600	3 - 40 DCF
247	71	365 Daytona	12 V	81 x 71	0,88	365,8	4390	9,3	350	7000	6 - 40 DCN
248	71	312 B-F I	12 B	78,5 x 51,5	0,66	249,3	2991	11,5	480	11.500	Lucas Inj.
249	71	312 P-Sport	12 B	78,5 x 51,5	0,66	249,3	2991	11,5	450	10.800	Lucas Inj.
250	71	246 Dino GT	6 V	92,5 x 60	0,65	403,1	2418,4	9	195	7600	3 - 40 DCF
251	71	512 M	12 V	87 x 70	0,8	416	4923	11,8	610	9000	Lucas Inj.
252	71	365 GT 2+2	12 V	81 x 71	0,88	365,8	4390,3	8,8	320	6600	3 - 40 DCN
253	71	365 GTC 4	12 V	81 x 71	0,88	365,8	4390,3	8,8	340	6800	6 - 40 DCOE
254	72	BB	12 B	81 x 71	0,88	365,8	4390	8,8	360	7500	4 - 40 IDL 3C
255	72	312 B2-F I	12 B	78,5 x 51,5	0,66	249,3	2991	11,5	480	11.800	Lucas Inj.
256	72	312 P	12 B	78,5 x 51,5	0,66	249,3	2991	11,5	450	10.800	Lucas Inj.
257	72	246 Dino GTS	6 V	92,5 x 60	0,65	403,1	2418,4	9	195	7600	3 - 40 DCF
258	72	246 Dino GT	6 V	92,5 x 60	0,65	403,1	2418,4	9	195	7600	3 - 40 DCF
259	72	365 GTB 4	12 V	81 x 71	0,88	365,8	4390	8,8	350	7000	6 - 40 DCOE
260	72	365 GTC 4	12 V	81 x 71	0,88	365,8	4390	8,8	320	6800	6 - 40 DCOE

Ignition: S = simple; D = double: B = reel; M = magneto. **Engine position:** A = Front; P = rear. **Gearbox position:** A = front; P = rear; V = overdrive. **Suspension:** B = springs; BT = transverse springs; M = coil springs; DD = De Dion bridge; O = swinging semiaxle; I = independent or transverse parallelogram; N = normal rigid bridge.

ignition	number of camshafts	engine position	gearbox position and number of speeds	wheelbase (mm)	front track (mm)	rear track (mm)	front suspensions	rear suspensions	front tires	rear tires	weight (kg)	capacity fuel tank (l)	maximum speed (kph)
ino ex	2	P	P 5	2220	1405	1400	I-M	I-M	5,00/9,50 x 13	6,00/12,50 x 13	425	130	300
ino ex	2	P	P 5	2370	1485	1500	I-M	I-M	4,75/10,30 x 15	6,00/13,50 x 15	680	120	320
2 B	1	A	A 5	2650	1438	1468	I-M	I-M	200 x 15	200 x 15	1580	100	245
ino ex Transverse	2	P	P 5	2340	1425	1400	I-M	I-M	185 x 14	185 x 14	1080	70	245
2 B	2	A	P 5	2400	1440	1425	I-M	I-M	200 x 15	200 x 15	1200	100	260
B	2	Experimental engine built with only 3 cylinders											
2 B	1	A	A 5	2400	1401	1417	I-M	I-M	205 x 14	205 x 14	1350	90	245
2 B	1	A	A 5	2400	1401	1417	I-M	I-M	205 x 14	205 x 14	1250	90	245
ino ex	2	P	P 5	2340	1377	1412	I-M	I-M	5,00/10 x 13	6,00/14 x 13	500	80	280
ino ex	2	P	P 4	2450	1603	1590	I-M	I-M	4,90/13,90 x 15	6,00/15,50 x 15	700	140	355
no ex	2	P	P 5	2400	1518	1511	I-M	I-M	4,25/11,50 x 11	6,00/14,50 x 15	820	140	340
no ex	2	P	P 5	2385	1586	1577	I-M	I-M	5,00/10 x 13	12,5/25 x 15	539	200	300
2 B	2	A	A 5	2650	1438	1468	I-M	I-M	200 x 15	200 x 15	1600	100	245
2 B	2	A	P 5	2400	1440	1425	I-M	I-M	200 x 15	200 x 15	1200	100	280
no ex Transverse	2	P	P 5	2340	1425	1430	I-M	I-M	205/70 VR x 14		1080	65	245
no ex	2	A	P 5	2400	1440	1425	I-M	I-M	200 x 15	200 x 15	1200	100	280
no ex	2	P	P 5	2385	1586	1597	I-M	I-M	5,00/10 x 13	12,5/25 x 15	534	200	300
no ex	2	P	P 5	2220	1425	1400	I-M	I-M	5,00/22 x 13	13/26 x 15	585	120	320
	2	P	P 5	2340	1425	1430	I-M	I-M	205/70 VR x 14		1080	65	245
no ex	2	P	P 5	2400	1518	1511	I-M	I-M	4,25/11,50 x 11	6,00/14,50 x 15	815	120	340
no ex	2	A	A 5	2650	1438	1468	I-M	I-M	200 x 15	200 x 15	1600	100	245
no ex	2	A	A 5	2500	1470	1470	I-M	I-M	215/70 x 15	215/70 x 15	1450	100	250
no ex	2	P	P 5	2500	1500	1500	I-M	I-M	215 x 15	215 x 15	1160	100	300
no ex	2	P	P 5	2385	1586	1597	I-M	I-M	9/20 x 13	13,24 x 13	550	220	300
no ex	2	P	P 5	2220	1425	1420	I-M	I-M	8,6/20 x 13	13,5/24 x 13	650	120	320
no ex	2	P	P 5	2340	1425	1430	I-M	I-M	205/70 VR x 14		1080	65	245
no ex	2	P	P 5	2340	1425	1430	I-M	I-M	205/70 VR x 14		1080	65	245
no ex	2	A	P 5	2400	1440	1425	I-M	I-M	215/70 x 15		1200	100	280
no x	2	A	A 5	2500	1470	1470	I-M	I-M	215/70 x 15		1400	100	260